SEASON OF SHATTERED DREAMS

SEASON OF SHATTERED DREAMS

POSTWAR BASEBALL, THE SPOKANE INDIANS, AND A TRAGIC BUS CRASH THAT CHANGED EVERYTHING

ERIC VICKREY

ROWMAN & LITTLEFIELD
Lanham • Boulder • New York • London

Published by Rowman & Littlefield
An imprint of The Rowman & Littlefield Publishing Group, Inc.
4501 Forbes Boulevard, Suite 200, Lanham, Maryland 20706
www.rowman.com

86-90 Paul Street, London EC2A 4NE, United Kingdom

British Library Cataloguing in Publication Information Available

Library of Congress Cataloging-in-Publication Data Available

ISBN 978-1-5381-9072-2 (cloth : alk. paper)
ISBN 978-1-5381-9073-9 (electronic)

∞™ The paper used in this publication meets the minimum requirements of American National Standard for Information Sciences—Permanence of Paper for Printed Library Materials, ANSI/NISO Z39.48-1992.

CONTENTS

PREFACE

When I first read about the Spokane Indians bus crash several years ago, the story stuck in the back of my mind. I am probably not alone in that regard. Once you know about the deadliest tragedy in the history of American professional sports, it is difficult to forget. The horrific 1946 accident made headlines in newspapers across the country in the ensuing days and has been chronicled on anniversaries in the decades since. But the story has largely faded from the collective conscience as the years have passed.

In addition to my interest in baseball history, the story captivated me because it took place in my adopted home of Washington State. I have driven over the same mountain pass where the crash occurred countless times. I became more intrigued as I learned about the team and events that unfolded that season as well as the years before and after. The Indians roster included an eclectic mix of players, a few of whom had already achieved success on grander stages. Ben Geraghty and Chris Hartje each flashed briefly with the Brooklyn Dodgers under Casey Stengel and Leo Durocher, respectively. Vic Picetti, the Indians' promising young first baseman, had rubbed elbows with future Hall of Famers Mel Ott and Richie Ashburn at an amateur all-star game and received tutelage from one-time National League MVP Dolph Camilli. Most members of the Spokane team were attempting to resurrect baseball careers following years of military service, each hoping to etch his name in baseball's annals and earn a good living. Jack Lohrke, whose life story is almost beyond imagination, would do just that. Others were robbed of their chance because of a catastrophe in the Cascade Mountains.

It surprised me to find that, aside from local newspaper articles and a book of fiction by Beth Mary Bollinger called *Until the End of the Ninth*, there had not been much written about the tragedy. I felt the players' stories deserved to be told, which is what I set out to do.

The events described in this book took place in the era of World War II, which shaped nearly every aspect of life at the time. Most of the men on Spokane's roster served in the military during the war, and many fought overseas in some its most grueling campaigns. Some of the players met their fate nearly eighty years ago and endure through grainy black-and-white photographs and anecdotes passed down through generations. A fortunate few lived into the twenty-first century and are vividly remembered in the hearts and minds of sons, daughters, nieces, nephews, and grandchildren.

This story is a culmination of research that went in many directions. The *Spokane Chronicle* and *Spokesman-Review* archives provided many of the day-to-day details. Articles in recent decades by Jim Price, a renowned Spokane baseball historian, were thorough and insightful. Information about Ben Geraghty was gleaned through books authored by Pat Jordan and Henry Aaron and firsthand accounts shared by several players he managed. Jack Lohrke's family offered memories and invaluable information about his life and career; relatives of several other players did the same. And Bob Paterson and Vic Picetti helped tell their own stories through letters that were pulled out of boxes and dusted off nearly eighty years after they wrote them by family they never met.

This is a story of hope, tragedy, inconceivable happenstance, and perseverance. And baseball is at the center of it all.

PROLOGUE

A ramshackle bus sputtered west out of Spokane, Washington, on the unseasonably chilly morning of June 24, 1946. Aboard were sixteen passengers, ranging in age from eighteen to thirty-three, who aspired to make a living playing baseball. They were members of a minor league team called the Spokane Indians. But this was no run-of-the-mill group of long-shot dreamers, and 1946 was no ordinary year. The United States had reabsorbed millions of demobilized servicemen and women since the end of World War II a year earlier. Instead of returning to prewar normalcy, however, Americans dealt with a housing shortage, scarcity of goods and services, and rising inflation. Meanwhile, wages failed to keep up with the skyrocketing cost of living. As a result, coal miners, meatpackers, railroad engineers, and workers in myriad other industries walked off their jobs. The national pastime provided Americans with a distraction from the country's stark reality.

Professional baseball faced a similar postwar influx. More than five hundred major leaguers and four thousand minor leaguers had swapped jerseys for military fatigues during the previous four years. Two former big leaguers, Harry O'Neill and Elmer Gedeon, plus more than one hundred minor-league players, lost their lives.[1] Many were now eager to resume their baseball careers. Some, such as Bob Feller, Hank Greenberg, and Ted Williams, had been prewar superstars and were out to reclaim their status among the game's elite. The majority, however, had been toiling in the minor leagues or on the cusp of stardom when they were called to serve. Yet another group of players—those who had kept the game afloat during the war—were anxious to prove they belonged.[2]

In the spring of 1946, major league training camps overflowed with players attempting to shake off rust and rediscover baseball skills put on the backburner during the war. The same could be said for the Pacific Coast League (PCL), which, in many ways, was the major league of the West Coast. Big league baseball had yet to expand west of St. Louis, so the PCL held top billing in cities such as Los Angeles, San Francisco, Oakland, and Seattle. Attendance and salaries in the PCL rivaled the majors, and the quality of play was only a tick below. The circuit was a desirable place to play, particularly for players who lived on the West Coast.

As a result of overcrowding in baseball's top tiers, many talented players were pushed to the lower levels of the minor leagues, including the Class B Western International League (WIL). Before the war, teams with a Class B designation were mostly made up of players in their teens or early twenties who had a slim chance of making the majors. But postwar, some of the PCL's best prospects were farmed out to make room for returning servicemen who were now in their late twenties and thirties. The Spokane Indians, an independent franchise in the WIL, were among the recipients of the overflow. The Indians were largely comprised of players who belonged to the New York Yankees and two PCL teams—the San Diego Padres and Oakland Oaks. The Indians' owner, Sam Collins, had formed working agreements with these three organizations as a means of obtaining players he hoped to mold into a league champion. After all, the primary objectives of minor league teams in the 1940s were winning and turning a profit rather than player development.

The Indians roster consisted of players from small towns, big cities, both coasts, the upper Midwest, a cowboy ranch in Arizona, and tribal land in Idaho. Many were second- and third-generation Americans whose parents or grandparents emigrated from Germany, Ireland, Scotland, Italy, Mexico, Poland, and Russia. Several had gained valuable experience playing for service teams during the war and held their own against major league competition. Some players, including Padres prospect Jack Lohrke, had put aside baseball while fighting in some of the war's deadliest battles. Ben Geraghty and Chris Hartje, both in their early thirties, previously had cups of coffee in the major leagues and were hanging on to fading playing careers.

Geraghty hoped to someday put the knowledge he acquired from Casey Stengel to use as a big league manager. And then there was Vic Picetti, an eighteen-year-old first baseman considered to be the best prospect on the West Coast and the latest in a long line of Italian American ballplayers to come out of San Francisco—a lineage that included names like DiMaggio, Lazzeri, and Camilli. As the sole supporter of his mother and two younger siblings, Picetti had a lot riding on his shoulders. The Indians had varying levels of promise and talent, but all shared a common goal of providing for their families and moving up to the PCL or, just maybe, the major leagues.

Through the first two months of the season, the Indians' play had been up and down. The team's pitching, aside from ace Milt Cadinha, had been shaky. Collins had cycled through several underperforming catchers before landing Hartje in mid-June. But the Indians sure could hit. Most of the infielders and outfielders had batting averages over .300, and several were among the league leaders. Spokane's robust offense meant that they were never out of a ballgame. Such was the case on June 23, 1946, when they came from behind in dramatic fashion to defeat the first-place Salem Senators.

The thrilling victory left the Indians in high spirits the next morning despite the arduous bus journey ahead. Their next series was in Bremerton, Washington, a navy town on the Kitsap Peninsula. Getting there required a road trip over Snoqualmie Pass in the Cascade Mountains. What started as a routine day in the lives of a minor league ball club turned catastrophic. By the end of the day, seven would be dead, eight would be hospitalized, and one would be hitchhiking back to Spokane.

1

LOHRKE

Jack Lohrke arrived at the embarkation point in the south of England during the early afternoon of July 6, 1944. He boarded the USS *LST-134*, a tank landing ship that stretched the length of a football field. Since D-Day a month earlier, the vessel had delivered Allied troops, artillery, and equipment to the beaches of Normandy in northern France. On return trips, it transported casualties.

At 6:30 p.m. a pair of 900-horsepower diesel engines roared as the *LST-134* pulled away from the dock. For the next twenty-one and a half hours, the ship churned across the choppy waters of the English Channel before landing at Omaha Beach. While Lohrke anxiously counted the hours, baseball carried on at Sportsman's Park in St. Louis, where the New York Giants clobbered the Cardinals, 10–1. By the time Lohrke stepped foot in France, the Giants had traveled to Chicago for a July 7 doubleheader versus the Cubs. The Giants' Mel Ott went seven for eight in the twin bill and blasted the 482nd home run of his storied career. Lohrke himself had dreams of playing in the big leagues someday. But on this day, baseball was the furthest thing from his mind.

Jack Wayne Lohrke was born on February 25, 1924, in Los Angeles, California. His father, John Lohrke, was born in Texas to German immigrants and married Marguerite Hurd, a native Michigander, in 1919. Jack was the second of three boys; Kenneth was three years older, and Robert two years younger. John, a World War I veteran, worked as a fruit packer at the public market and then later as an assemblyman. Marguerite was a homemaker. When Jack was young, the family lived in a tiny two-bedroom bungalow in the Firestone Park neighborhood of Los Angeles. Later, they upgraded to a modest three-bedroom home in nearby Bell.

Lohrke grew up playing softball and took a liking to baseball as a teenager. At fifteen, he attended a White Sox training school and worked out as a catcher.[1] He attended South Gate High but did not go out for the baseball team. His parents, who instilled a strong work ethic in Jack, required him to pick fruit and help out with chores after school, leaving no time for baseball during the school year. When Lohrke was old enough to work, he got a job changing lightbulbs on the marquee of a neighborhood movie theater. Despite missing out on the experience of playing high school ball, Jack possessed enough raw talent at age sixteen to occasionally play shortstop for a semipro team called the East Pasadena Merchants. After he graduated from South Gate in 1941, Lohrke focused more of his attention on baseball. Jack Tolliver, a scout with the San Diego Padres of the PCL, saw him on the semipro circuit and signed him to a contract in the spring of 1942.

By then, the United States was embroiled in World War II, but the Pacific Coast League, like major league baseball, had carried on with the encouragement of President Franklin D. Roosevelt, who foresaw the benefit that baseball could have on morale. In a letter to Commissioner Kenesaw Mountain Landis dated January 14, 1942, Roosevelt wrote, "I honestly feel that it would be best for the country to keep baseball going. There will be fewer people unemployed, and everybody will work longer hours and harder than ever before. And that means that they ought to have a chance for recreation and for taking their minds off their work even more than before."[2] Roosevelt's "green light" letter paved the way for baseball to forge ahead through the war. More night games were scheduled so factory workers could attend, and troops overseas kept up with the sport by reading *The Sporting News* and listening to broadcasts on shortwave radio.

Lohkre grew to be five-feet-eleven and 180 pounds with a tree-trunk neck and solid build. He was strikingly handsome, with dark brown hair, arched eyebrows, a square jaw, and a wide smile. On the baseball field, he had a cannon for an arm and could have been a pitcher had he not been such a good infielder.

At his first spring training with the Padres in 1942, Lohrke got a taste of big league competition, starting both games of a doubleheader versus the Pittsburgh Pirates while the regular third baseman, Art Garibaldi, sat out because of a salary dispute.[3] Jack was hitless that day but attracted attention with his "sparkling" defense.[4] Because of a smattering of injuries to the Padres' more veteran players, Lohrke made the team out of spring training and saw action early in the regular season. The *San Diego Union* wrote that he "fielded his position like a veteran" and "won the hearts of the fans with hustle and fighting spirit."[5] Once the veteran players got healthy, the Padres optioned Lohrke to the Twin Falls Cowboys so he could gain experience against players his age. In the southern Idaho town, he hit .271 with three home runs while splitting his time between third base and shortstop. One of Lohrke's teammates on the Cowboys was Nick Sunseri, a fellow Angeleno. Nick introduced Jack to his sister, Marie, and the pair hit it off.

Lohrke's pursuit of a baseball career and Marie were put on pause that winter. He was inducted into the army on February 5, 1943, and assigned to the Thirty-Fifth Infantry, 216th Field Artillery Battalion, Battery A. The Thirty-Fifth Infantry Division, known as the Santa Fe Division, had roots in World War I, when many of its men came from states along the Santa Fe Trail. The newly enlisted men of the Thirty-Fifth underwent months of rigorous combat training before moving to Tennessee, where they spent two months in cold, damp weather performing maneuvers designed to simulate battle conditions they would soon face overseas. On January 18, 1944, they moved to Camp Butner, North Carolina, for their final rounds of training and preparation.

On May 12, 1944, the 216th Field Artillery Battalion embarked on the USAT *Edmund B. Alexander*, which steamed out of the New York Port of Embarkation.[6] Thirteen days and more than three thousand miles later, they arrived in England. The soldiers traveled by train through the English countryside, passing rolling emerald hills and thatched-roof houses. Interspersed among the idyllic scene were pockmarked churches and piles of rubble from years of German shelling. The 216th took up barracks in the southwest England town of Okehampton, where they awaited deployment to northern France. The Santa Fe Division was now a part of General Patton's Third Army.

General Dwight D. Eisenhower, the supreme commander of the Allied Expeditionary Forces, visited Okehampton on the morning of June 25 and inspected Lohrke's battalion.[7] Ike was satisfied with what he saw. Days later, the 216th was ordered to waterproof their equipment. They would soon be moving to a marshalling area in preparation for the voyage to Normandy.

The *LST-134* carrying Lohrke landed on Omaha Beach at 16:00 on July 7.[8] Since the D-Day invasion thirty-one days earlier, Allied forces had fiercely battled to secure the beachheads of Normandy and the port town of Cherbourg. The next objective was to capture Saint-Lô, a city twenty-five miles south of Omaha Beach that had tactical importance as the region's transportation hub. Getting there required the Allied forces to fight the Nazis in rolling fields checkered with dense hedgerows and drainage ditches. The challenging terrain provided the enemy with natural defenses and rendered Allied tanks useless.

On July 10, Lohrke's battalion set up their guns—105-mm howitzers that weighed nearly five thousand pounds and could fire at a range of up to seven miles. For the next week they provided artillery support for the 320th Infantry Regiment as they hacked through the dense vegetation. The Allies slowly inched forward before finally securing Saint-Lô on July 20—the same day as a failed assassination attempt on Adolf Hitler by the German resistance. The Thirty-Fifth Division, already scarred and battle tested, emerged victorious. But for Jack and his comrades, this was just the beginning.

By early December, the Allies had liberated Paris and the Thirty-Fifth Division had advanced east across France. Farther north, Allied forces had gained control of the vital port of Antwerp, Belgium, and were poised along the German border in the Belgian and Luxembourg Ardennes Forest. Some Allied leaders believed the European war would be over by Christmas. But then on December 16, the Germans launched a last-ditch counteroffensive through the weakly defended Ardennes in an attempt to split British and American forces. The Battle of the Bulge had begun.

Lohrke's battalion was stationed in Wiesviller, France, near the German border, when the Nazis launched the Ardennes campaign. Hitler and his generals believed the Americans would quickly retreat to the Meuse River to set up defense. Instead of causing panic and collapse, however, the attack provoked steadfast resistance by the Allies, including staunch defense of the key Belgian city of Bastogne, along the southern shoulder of the offensive. The Germans planned to use the network of roads in Bastogne to hasten their advance, and by December 21 they had the town surrounded. In the meantime, temperatures had plummeted, and snow blanketed the region. For several days, clouds and fog prohibited the delivery of much-needed food, ammunition, medical supplies, and fuel to American troops, who desperately clung to Bastogne and slowed the German advance despite being ill-prepared for the weather. Some soldiers used burlap sacks in an attempt to warm freezing feet. Camouflage vehicles and uniforms now stood out in the pearly white snow, so troops scoured the area for white bedsheets and paint to make themselves less conspicuous. The Germans delivered an ultimatum on December 22: surrender or face annihilation. Brigadier General Anthony McAuliffe famously gave a one-word reply: "Nuts!"[9] The next day, clear skies allowed Allied planes to deliver supplies to the trapped units. The tide of the battle began to turn. German commanders soon realized the stalled offensive was doomed to fail and advised withdrawal, but Hitler refused to admit defeat and instead ordered further attacks on Christmas Day.

Lohrke spent a blustery Christmas morning in Metz, France, enjoying a turkey dinner and his first bit of rest since landing on Omaha Beach more than five months earlier.[10] The downtime was brief, however. That night, the Santa Fe Division received orders to move eighty miles north to Belgium to help relieve the encircled American troops in Bastogne. Within twenty-four hours, Lohrke's unit was in the thick of the Battle of the Bulge.

The Santa Fe became one of twenty-two infantry divisions embroiled in the fighting as the calendar turned to 1945. Nearly a half million Allied troops shifted to the Ardennes. As a fire control man in the 216th Field Artillery Battalion, Lohrke's duties included compiling firing data with instruments such as an aiming circle, telescope, and compass, as well as using a graphical firing table slide rule to help his battery conduct artillery fire. Field artillery battalions mostly performed long-range shelling but were sometimes used to halt tank assaults on the front lines.

The brutal battle continued in freezing temperatures and waist-deep snow. On one occasion, Lohrke, frigid from the bitter cold and exhausted from endless fighting, fell asleep standing next to a haystack.[11] Many troops fell victim to trench foot and frostbite. Cecil Travis, a star infielder with the

Washington Senators before the war, fought in Ardennes Forest as part of the Seventy-Sixth Infantry Division. "Heck, you was in that snow, and you was out in that weather, and if you was lucky you got to stay in an old barn at night," recalled Travis. "The thing about it, you'd sit there in those boots, and you might not get 'em off for days at a time. And cold! You'd just shake at night. Your feet would start swelling, and that's how you'd find out there was something really wrong—you'd pull your boots off, and your feet is swelling."[12] Travis developed frostbite that required emergency surgery to his left foot. He returned to baseball after the war but was never the same player he had been and retired at age thirty-four.

The Battle of the Bulge, as described by historian Antony Beevor, "reached a degree of savagery unprecedented on the western front."[13] Besides bloodshed on the front lines, there was a massacre of eighty-four American prisoners of war in Malmedy and the indiscriminate killing of countless Belgian citizens. The Allies emerged victorious after six weeks, but the battle proved costly. The Americans suffered more than 75,000 casualties in the Ardennes campaign, including 8,407 killed, making it the bloodiest battle of the war.[14]

The Thirty-Fifth Division continued on to Holland and then Germany through the final days of Hitler's reign. All told, Lohrke's unit traveled roughly sixteen hundred miles after landing in Normandy. The 216th Field Artillery Battalion fired one of the last shots of the European theater at 2:05 p.m. on April 27.[15] Eleven days later, Germany officially surrendered.

The battle-weary Santa Fe Division next performed occupational duties in Koblenz, Germany. Compared to the endless fighting of the previous ten months, it was a relaxing assignment. Some troops took the opportunity to enjoy a few days of leave in Paris or Switzerland. Others took part in the division's expansive athletic program, which included an entry in the four-team Fifteenth Army Baseball League. The Thirty-Fifth Division team was called the Santa Fe Indians and played their home games in a stadium first built by the American Army of Engineers in 1920 during the United States' occupation of the area following World War I. The stadium had reverted to German control at the end of the decade. In 1932, it was the site of an Adolf Hitler rally in which he implored a crowd of fifteen thousand Germans to reelect him under a promise of lasting peace. The Nazi Party renamed the stadium after military leader Hermann Göring and constructed a new grandstand and bleachers in conjunction with the 1936 Olympics. It was significantly damaged from Allied bombing and rebuilt with a baseball field by army engineers and prisoners after the Nazi regime fell.[16]

On July 1, 1945, the renovated ballpark was dedicated as Santa Fe Stadium during a pregame ceremony before the Indians played against the 106th Division Cubs. Murry Dickson, a pitcher with the 1942 World Champion St. Louis Cardinals, who drove the point Jeep of a Thirty-Fifth Division reconnaissance group, took the mound for the Indians. Jack Lohrke batted cleanup and played third base. The Indians defeated the Cubs that day, 5–2.[17]

Lohrke spent one year, eight months, and eleven days serving overseas during the war. He received numerous decorations, including the Good Conduct, American Campaign, Eastern Campaign, and Victory Medals. For the rest of his life, Jack rarely talked about his time in the military, even to family and close friends. If a reporter asked about the war years later, he would provide only the briefest of anecdotes. In one interview, Jack recalled the time he was reunited with his brother, Kenneth, on a battlefield in Maastricht, Holland.[18] Other reports through the years cited that on multiple occasions the man next to Lohrke on the battlefield was killed. He preferred not to relive such traumatic experiences and humbly downplayed his service. "I wasn't exactly Sergeant York," Lohrke once told *Sports Illustrated*. "My father didn't want heroes in our family."[19]

Private First Class Lohrke sailed back to the United States on the *Queen Mary* and arrived in New York on September 10, 1945.[20] A few days later, he excitedly waited to take the first flight of his life back home to California. At the last minute, however, a higher ranking serviceman bumped Lohrke off the plane, much to his chagrin. The Douglas C-47 transport aircraft took off without him and later stopped to refuel at Fairfax Municipal Airport near Kansas City.[21] Just after midnight on September 15, the plane departed Kansas City to complete the second leg of the trip. Minutes after takeoff, it crashed on the north bank of the Missouri River, killing the crew and twenty veterans who served in the European theater.[22]

Less than two weeks after he stepped back on American soil, Lohrke suited up for a Pasadena semipro team called the Chamberlain Athletics. He recorded four hits in six at-bats and cleanly fielded all five defensive chances at shortstop. One of his hits was a tiebreaking grand slam.[23] Lohrke had survived the war while seeing fellow servicemen killed, narrowly averted a plane crash, and was on a new mission: to play in the major leagues.

2

GERAGHTY

Both the weather and Casey Stengel's mood could be described as gloomy on one particular early spring day in March 1943. The fifty-two-year-old manager of the Boston Braves had good reason to be down in the dumps. With little more than a month until the first game of the regular season, he learned that his left fielder, Nanny Fernandez, had been drafted by Uncle Sam, further depleting an already thin Braves roster. Infielders Max West, Sibby Sisti, and Buddy Gremp had all enlisted, as had pitchers Tom Earley, Warren Spahn, and Johnny Sain. To make matters worse for Stengel, his star catcher, Ernie Lombardi, threatened to sit out the season to work at a defense plant unless he received a substantial raise. The Braves' money-strapped majority owner, J. A. Robert Quinn, ultimately traded Lombardi—the defending National League batting champion—to the New York Giants. The outlook for the upcoming campaign was even bleaker than usual for the Braves, perennial bottom-feeders who hadn't won a pennant in twenty-nine years.

Baseball's wartime manpower shortage forced teams to rely on players who were too young for the draft, past their playing prime, or exempt from military service. By 1943, the major leagues had lost 195 players to the military—an average of 12 players per team.[1] Only ten minor leagues remained in operation—down from forty-four before the war—leaving fewer sources of talent for big league teams. For some players, the circumstances provided a chance to resuscitate careers that had seemingly flatlined.

CHAPTER 2

Though baseball would continue during wartime, government officials urged Commissioner Landis to restrict unnecessary travel as a means of rationing oil and gas. As a result, he required that major league teams hold spring training north of the Mason-Dixon Line and east of the Mississippi River. The Braves chose Choate School, a prestigious college preparatory academy in Wallingford, Connecticut, which provided dormitory housing and an indoor facility where the Braves could throw and hit in batting cages. In order to get in practice games, the team sometimes played high schoolers on snow-covered ballfields. On one occasion, pitcher Lefty Gomez, attempting to extend his career in spite of a sore arm, played in a fur coat.[2] Connecticut was far from the sunshine of Florida, but many of the players' contemporaries faced far more grueling circumstances on the war front, so they had no room to complain. Stengel tried to look on the bright side; players would get in shape because they had to run just to stay warm.

The Braves scraped together a few options to compete for the third-base job. In addition to thirty-five-year-old second baseman Tony Cuccinello and converted catcher Mike Sandlock, they signed Joe Burns, a former minor leaguer who most recently had been reading meters for a Pennsylvania water company. Before Burns left for camp, he told his wife, "If I meet any guy who tries to take that third base job away from me, I'll break his arm."[3] Stengel also lured Ben Geraghty, one of his former players from his days managing the Brooklyn Dodgers. Geraghty had burst on the major league scene as a rookie straight out of Villanova University in 1936. He was the sensation of Dodgers spring camp and one of the best hitters in the league for the first two weeks of the regular season. Geraghty's rise to stardom faded quickly, however. Within a few years, he was working in a cemetery before taking a wartime defense plant job on the West Coast. Stengel, desperate for quality players after losing so many to the military, paid Geraghty a visit during the offseason and convinced him to travel east in the spring to try out for a spot on the Braves' roster. Burns walked back his threat of assault when he found out he would he competing with Geraghty. "I guess I won't break his arm after all," he said. "Ben's too nice a guy."[4]

Benjamin Raymond Geraghty was born on July 19, 1912, in Jersey City, New Jersey. He was the youngest of eight children born to Patrick and Ida (née Hines) Geraghty. The family lived at 157 Grand Street in a brick rowhouse a few blocks east of the Hudson River across from Lower Manhattan. The neighborhood was mostly comprised of working-class German, Irish, and Italian families who had sailed to America in search of a better life. Patrick, the son of Irish immigrants, worked as a teamster with a packing company and then as a driver for a tea factory before landing a night shift manager position at the National Grocery Company garage. Ida, also of Irish lineage, was a homemaker. On one August night in 1926, Patrick towed a stalled truck during a shift at the garage. While trying to unhitch the tow chain, the broken-down vehicle lunged forward, pinning him between the two trucks and killing him instantly.[5] Ben was only fourteen at the time. His older brother, Thomas, a police officer and strict disciplinarian, became the head of the household and Ben's surrogate father.

Ben was brown-haired and blue-eyed with a narrow face, thick eyebrows, hawk nose, and long chin. He loved sports growing up and got the most out of his slight frame on the athletic fields. He split his high school years between St. Peter's Preparatory School in Jersey City and St. Benedict's in Newark. Though he played football and baseball, Geraghty stood out at basketball. As a senior, he earned first-team All-State honors as a forward for the St. Benedict cagers.[6]

In the fall of 1932, Geraghty enrolled at Villanova University, where he continued to compete on the baseball diamond and basketball hardwood. He paid his tuition with money earned washing windows, scrubbing the gymnasium floor, and cleaning lockers.[7] Nicknamed "Bullet Ben" because of his quickness on the basketball court, Geraghty starred as a sharpshooting forward for the Wildcats. The *Philadelphia Inquirer* called Geraghty "one of Villanova's outstanding athletes in years" during his junior year.[8] Come spring, he played shortstop for the Villanova nine and posted a .379 batting average.[9] During his senior year of 1935 to 1936, Brooklyn Dodgers scout Mel Logan talked Geraghty into signing a contract. Geraghty captained the Wildcats basketball team despite having a professional baseball pact but feared injury and loafed on the court. His lack of effort resulted in fisticuffs with teammates after what would be his final college hoops game.[10]

Geraghty reported to Dodgers camp in Clearwater, Florida, in March 1936 and made a strong first impression on Stengel, who was entering his third season as Brooklyn's skipper. Geraghty caught a break early on when the incumbent shortstop, Lonnie Frey, contracted tonsillitis. Geraghty seized the opportunity and became the talk of camp with his terrific play. His spring was not without tribulation, however. He fell asleep in the sun one day between morning and afternoon workouts and suffered burns to his face that made it difficult to smile, talk, and eat.[11] Despite the minor setback, Geraghty played sparkling defense and recorded ten hits in his first twenty-seven spring at-bats, outplaying fellow shortstop Johnny Hudson and cementing a spot on Stengel's opening day roster. The dethroned Frey transitioned to second base after he recovered from his throat infection. Tommy Holmes of the *Brooklyn Daily Eagle* wrote that Geraghty's batting stance and glovework reminded him of erstwhile New York Giants infielder Glenn Wright.[12] Ironically, Geraghty and Wright would cross paths a decade later in Spokane, Washington.

Geraghty's jump from college to the major leagues was reminiscent of Frankie Frisch, star infielder-turned-manager of the St. Louis Cardinals. In Florida, Geraghty impressed Frisch, who warned not to overhype players based on meaningless spring games. "The older fellows really don't put on the pressure until April," said Frisch. "Geraghty can field, and he acts a fellow who won't be a lamb once he gets enough shots at big-league pitching . . . perhaps Geraghty is no flash in the pan."[13]

Geraghty missed the Dodgers' opening series at the Polo Grounds because of a sprained ankle and sore arm. The twenty-three-year-old instead made his debut in the Dodgers' home opener on April 17 versus the Phillies. Temperatures in the forties kept many folks away; the announced crowd was only 7,381—the lowest ever for an opener at Ebbets Field. Those who braved the elements witnessed an outstanding debut by Brooklyn's rookie shortstop. Geraghty, a so-called Punch-and-Judy hitter, singled, doubled, scored a run, and drove in another against future All-Star hurler Bucky Walters in the Dodgers' 4–3 victory. Four days later, Geraghty lashed three hits in as many at-bats against the Boston Bees (the franchise previously and later known as the Braves), starting a string of four consecutive multi-hit efforts. Through his first ten games, he recorded fifteen hits in thirty-five at-bats for a .429 average.

Geraghty worked doggedly on his defense, which had become a strength in his young career. "Every day the Dodgers were home I reached the park at 10 a.m., and when I arrived Stengel grabbed a fungo bat and hit grounders to me," Geraghty later recalled. "I fielded them for four hours a day without a letup. When Stengel wasn't hitting to me, [coaches] Otto Miller and Chick Fraser was. I used to see grounders in my sleep. What progress I have made is due to constant practice Stengel gave me. I must have fielded a million grounders."[14]

Geraghty hurt the thumb on his throwing hand while diving back to first base, an injury that interrupted his hot start.[15] The sore phalange swelled to the size of an onion and kept him out of action for a week.[16] When he returned to the lineup, Geraghty failed to recapture his previous offensive success. He managed only nine hits in his next seventy-nine at-bats—a batting average of only .114.

The offensive struggles humbled Geraghty, who looked around and realized that he lacked the raw talent of his peers. "I knew, the first month I was in with Brooklyn, that I was not good enough to play this game," he said years later. "I made up my mind that if I was going to stay in baseball, I'd have to do it with my head."[17] Armed with this realization, Geraghty sought to improve his baseball acumen, and there were few in the game more knowledgeable than Stengel.

Charles Dillon Stengel, known as Casey because he hailed from Kansas City, is best known for his unique personality and managerial exploits, though he had a solid fourteen-year playing career as an outfielder with the Dodgers, Pirates, Phillies, Giants, and Braves. He achieved a lifetime .284 average, won three pennants, and cracked two game-winning round-trippers in the 1923 World Series. Stengel's quirky sense of humor and mischievous antics largely overshadowed his on-field success, however. As a player, he possessed a fierce competitive spirit, which manifested in bench-jockeying and fights with umpires and opponents. Stengel was also an entertainer. He would pantomime entire speeches, mimic opposing pitchers' windups, and regale the press with his own unique vocabulary and double-talk, which writers termed "Stengelese." One of his more memorable stunts came as a member of the Pirates in 1919, shortly after the Dodgers traded him away. Stengel was playing outfield that day but after the sixth inning decided to pay a visit to his former teammates in the Dodgers' bullpen. Brooklyn reliever Leon Cadore, who was deft at sleight-of-hand magic, caught an injured sparrow that had flown into a wall. Stengel placed the bird under his cap, where it remained until his next at-bat. As Stengel biographer Marty Appel described in *Casey Stengel: Baseball's*

Greatest Character, "Casey proceeded to face the fans, and in one motion, took a deep bow and removed his cap, permitting the now recovered sparrow to fly off."[18]

But underneath Stengel's clownish exterior was a tremendous understanding of baseball strategy and a keen ability to teach younger players—a skill set he picked up playing for Hall of Fame managers Wilbert Robinson and John McGraw. Stengel, who had floppy ears, deep face wrinkles, and a gravelly voice, developed an incredible eye for subtleties that he used to his advantage. "He could tell if a fastball was coming by how quickly the pitcher was chewing his tobacco, or by how wide the third baseman opened his eyes," wrote Appel.[19]

Geraghty seized the opportunity to learn from Stengel. He hung around the sage skipper late at night after games, absorbing bits of knowledge like a dog waiting for a morsel. Geraghty had obtained a journalism degree from Villanova, and now he was getting his master's degree in baseball from the "Old Perfessor," as Stengel was known. Geraghty's time in the big leagues was brief, however. His weak bat ultimately cost him his starting job and then his spot on the Dodgers' roster. On August 1, the Dodgers sent Geraghty to a minor league affiliate in Allentown, Pennsylvania, where he spent the remainder of the season.

That offseason, Geraghty lost control of his car and struck a tree while driving through Hanover, New Jersey, on a rainy night. He suffered torn muscles and ligaments to his throwing arm, an injury that lingered into the next season.[20] The Dodgers assigned the lame-armed infielder to their farm team in Knoxville, Tennessee, for the 1937 season, but Geraghty failed to report so the Dodgers placed him on the ineligible list.[21] In August, Brooklyn traded Geraghty to the Washington Senators. His rights now belonged to Trenton—a Senators Class A farm team. That December, Commissioner Landis reinstated Geraghty, who spent the offseason in New Jersey working as a cemetery superintendent, overseeing a crew of twenty men.[22] He returned to the ball diamond in 1938, hitting .264 for Trenton in 120 games. Later that year, he married fellow New Jersey native Mary Dowd.

Geraghty worked out with the Senators in the spring of 1939 before being sent to their minor league affiliate in Springfield, Massachusetts, where he registered a .233 batting average in thirty-six games before suffering a season-ending elbow dislocation.[23] He returned to his cemetery job and spent the summer of 1940 playing semipro ball in Brooklyn. For all intents and purposes, Geraghty's professional career was over.

During the war, Geraghty moved to California and took job at an airplane plant. For fifteen months, he worked from 11:30 p.m. to 10:00 a.m. for $100 per week—a good income at the time.[24] But Stengel had a third-base opening and thought highly enough of Geraghty to invite him to Braves' camp. After being out of professional baseball for nearly four years, forfeiting a secure paycheck for a non-roster invitation was a gamble Geraghty was willing to take. In March 1943, he traveled across the country to the idyllic town of Wallingford and the ivy-covered walls of Choate School.

Geraghty's skin was pale, and his face had thinned from months of working night shifts and long hours. Seven years removed from his first big league camp, his bat was rusty, and he missed more ground balls than he used to. To make matters worse, he was sidelined for several days of practice, first from a basketball-related injury and then from taking a bad-hop ground ball to the eye.[25] Still, Geraghty showed Stengel flashes of his younger form and made the cut for the Braves' opening day roster as a backup infielder.

Five days before the start of the regular season, Stengel crossed Commonwealth Avenue in Boston on a stormy night. He had his raincoat pulled up over his face and failed to see an approaching car, whose headlights were partially covered due to wartime blackout rules. Stengel's right leg took the brunt of the impact, resulting in severe fractures of his tibia and fibula. He was placed in traction for a week until the swelling subsided enough for him to undergo an extensive surgery to piece together the shattered bones. Bob Coleman filled in as interim manager until Stengel returned to the dugout with crutches on June 18. Geraghty, meanwhile, spent the first three months of the season with Boston but rarely saw the field. He batted only once and made a smattering of appearances as a pinch runner and defensive replacement. In July, the Braves optioned him to the Hartford Bees of the Class A Eastern League, where he posted a .312 batting average in thirty-nine games.

By 1944, the number of major leaguers in the service had ballooned to around 340. Several thousand minor leaguers had also joined the war effort. For thirty-one-year-old Ben Geraghty, that meant an opportunity to extend his playing career. He returned to Choate for another spring training and competed with twenty-four-year-old Connie Ryan for the second-base job. He would not be playing for Stengel, however. Boston had failed to finish higher than fifth place during Stengel's six years at the helm, and the Braves' new owner, Lou Perini, wanted a new manager. Stengel resigned before Perini could fire him and was replaced by Coleman.

Geraghty appeared to have a leg up for the starting second-base job in Wallingford, but a bout of arthritis forced him out of action for a chunk of camp and pushed him to the bench. He made the opening day roster for the second straight season but only appeared in seven games before being farmed out to Syracuse. The Braves recalled Geraghty in September and he played in four more games, finishing the season with four hits in sixteen at-bats. That would prove to be the end of his major-league career. In 146 career at-bats, Geraghty compiled a .199 batting average, .245 on-base percentage, and managed only four extra-base hits—all doubles.

Geraghty began the 1945 season with the Braves, who optioned him to the Double-A Indianapolis Indians before he ever appeared in a game. He served as the Indians' leadoff man and defensive stalwart at the keystone, hitting a solid .270 while committing only thirteen errors in 117 games.

The Sacramento Solons of the Pacific Coast League viewed Geraghty as second-base insurance and purchased his contract from Indianapolis for the 1946 season. In the Golden State, Geraghty avoided the housing shortage plaguing the nation by staying at the home of former Braves teammate Manny Salvo. Geraghty's time in Sacramento was brief, however. He seldom played during the first month of the season and was released in early May when team executives looked to shed payroll and use younger players. Nearing his thirty-fourth birthday, it became clear to Geraghty that his playing days were winding down. He had carved out a niche in the game on hustle and guile. In the entirety of his professional career—which would culminate in 2,168 plate appearances—Geraghty never hit a home run. But he knew the game inside and out. And he thought about following in the footsteps of Stengel and putting his acumen to use as a manager once the right opportunity presented itself.

3

PICETTI

All I want to do is play ball, and I certainly am lucky to have the chance.

—Vic Picetti[1]

What Ben Geraghty lacked in power and raw ability, Vic Picetti possessed in spades. Scouts described him as a can't-miss prospect and practically tripped over each other to sign him. It was not a question of *if* Picetti would make the major leagues, but how great he would become.

Vic's father, Victor Gasper Picetti (pronounced Pi-Chetti) was born in Genoa, Italy, shortly after the turn of the twentieth century. As a toddler, Victor and his family boarded a passenger ship in Havre, France. Eleven days later, they were greeted by the Statue of Liberty in New York City.[2] The Picettis made their way three thousand miles west, joining an enclave of fellow Italian immigrants in San Francisco's Mission District. Victor quickly developed a love for America's national pastime, competing on local sandlots as a player and then a manager.

The Genoese in the Bay Area often got together for potlucks and picnics, which is where Victor met his future bride, Angela Barrachi. Both came from Genoa, though their families had never mingled back in the old country. Victor and Angela welcomed a son, Victor Andrew, on July 20, 1927. Instead of a rattle, the elder Victor put a baseball in his son's hand.[3]

The family eventually grew to five with the additions of Beverly in 1931 and Robert in 1943. They lived at 60 Benton Avenue, a two-bedroom, one-bath home on a sloped street in the south end of the Mission. Vic Sr. worked as a garbage collector for Sunset Scavenger Company; Angela was a homemaker.

Vic Jr., known to his family as Junior, started playing organized baseball at age ten in the Catholic Youth Organization.[4] Baseball was everything to the youngster. His bedroom walls were adorned with pictures of major league stars, including his favorite player—Dolph Camilli of the Brooklyn Dodgers. Dolph served as natural role model for Vic. Both were of Italian heritage, born in San Francisco, and left-handed first basemen.

Vic had dark brown curly hair, almond-colored eyes, prominent cheeks, and a strong jawline. He played baseball at both Horace Mann Junior High and then Mission High School, whose entire season consisted of only nine games, and spent his summers during high school suiting up for the Rincon Hill American Legion ball team. In 1942, he led Rincon Hill in hitting with a .445 average.[5] The following year, he led the squad to the national championship tournament in Billings, Montana, where they lost to the eventual champions from Minneapolis.

As a junior in 1944, Picetti hit .406, won all-city honors, and propelled the Mission High Bears to the city championship.[6] By then, he was widely regarded as one of the top prep players on the West Coast. Just a shade under six feet tall, his solid build and mature face easily could have allowed him to pass as a decade older. Dozens of major league and Pacific Coast League scouts visited the Picetti house, each clamoring to sign Vic to a professional contract. One team, however, could offer more than just money and fame. Just across the bay, the Oakland Oaks employed Vic's hero as a player-manager.

Dolph Camilli's parents were Italian immigrants lured to San Francisco by the opportunity for steady work as the city rebuilt from the devastating 1906 earthquake. His father's drinking and domestic abuse eventually tore the family apart, however, forcing Dolph to spend parts of his teenage years living in a grocery store storage closet and a Catholic Church.[7] He developed into an excellent ballplayer despite his difficult upbringing, turning pro at age nineteen and rising to prominence in the Pacific Coast League (PCL)—first with his hometown Seals and then the Sacramento Senators—before signing with the Chicago Cubs in 1933. A year later, he was dealt to the Philadelphia Phillies, where in three full seasons he averaged twenty-seven home runs. Before the 1938 campaign, the Phillies traded Camilli to the lowly Brooklyn Dodgers, who had finished in the bottom half of the National League standings in sixteen of the previous twenty-one seasons.

The acquisition of Camilli and hiring of Leo Durocher as manager in 1939 helped turn the Dodgers' fortunes. Camilli, a quiet and gentle man, let his bat do the talking. He had a muscular five-feet-ten, 185-pound frame, and his vicious left-handed swing was well-suited for Ebbets Field, where the right-field foul pole stood 297 feet from home plate. With the contribution of Camilli's league-high thirty-four home runs and 120 RBIs, the Dodgers won a franchise-record one hundred games in 1941 and captured the National League pennant before losing to Joe DiMaggio and the New York Yankees in the World Series. Camilli's outstanding season earned him the National League Most Valuable Player Award.

By 1943, Camilli's productivity had waned. The Dodgers' new general manager, Branch Rickey, traded him midseason to Brooklyn's crosstown rivals, the New York Giants. Camilli refused to report to his new team. "I hated the Giants," he later explained. "This was real serious; this was no put-on stuff. Their fans hated us, and our fans hated them. I said nuts to them, and I quit."[8] The thirty-six-year-old father of five spent the rest of the summer working on his 1,750-acre cattle ranch in Northern California.

After the 1943 season, theater owners Clarence "Brick" Laws and Joe Blumenfeld bought the Oakland Oaks. They wanted to make splash and offered Babe Ruth the team's managerial position, but he declined. Camilli, still under contract with the Giants, declared his interest in the job. That winter, the Oaks traded the rights to Bill Rigney to the Giants for Camilli, who agreed to play and manage in Oakland for the next two seasons.

Picetti was one of thirty high schoolers selected for an all-star game in June 1944 that pitted against each other the best players from each side of the bay. It was not just an exhibition, however. *Esquire* magazine organized an East versus West All-American Boys' Game that was scheduled to take place at the Polo Grounds in New York on August 7. Northern California had to choose one representative for the all-expenses-paid trip. That player would be selected from the Bay Area all-star game participants by a panel of judges. Weeks before the contest, sportswriters Clyde Giraldo and Bob Marcus predicted that Picetti would run away with the vote.[9] The game was played on June 25 at Seals Stadium in front of seven thousand spectators. A group of fourteen judges included former big leaguers Tony Lazzeri and Bill Lange, Stanford University baseball coach Harry Wolter, Reds scout Mickey Shader, and several local high school coaches. Each ranked their top three choices. Three points were awarded for a first place vote, two for second, and one for third.[10]

Most of the youngsters played with a nervousness that contributed to a combined nine errors between the two teams.[11] One player seemingly unfazed by the stakes of the game was Picetti, described by the *San Francisco Chronicle* as "the coolest head on the field."[12] The phenom doubled twice, put down a successful sacrifice bunt, stole a base, and played flawless defense. One of his two-baggers came off a southpaw's curveball, the other against a righty's fastball.[13] Picetti also demonstrated a bit of leadership, calming down his pitcher during a pressure-filled moment. "He even wears his uniform like a major leaguer," remarked Marcus, who had the honor of announcing the All-American representative following the game's conclusion.[14] When Marcus declared Picetti as the winner with twenty-three votes, the other players cheered and offered congratulations. Vic's parents cried tears of joy. His father recognized the amazing opportunity afforded to his son and said he would have given ten years' salary to have had the same opportunity when he was sixteen.[15]

Picetti spent the weeks leading up to the All-American game playing American Legion ball and working out with Camilli and the Oaks. Picetti and Camilli had a mutual admiration. Vic considered Dolph to be the best first baseman in the game, while Camilli declared that Picetti was "the greatest prospect I ever saw come straight out of high school."[16]

Picetti made the long journey to New York by train, accompanied by *San Francisco Chronicle* reporter Bill Leiser, who referred to himself as Vic's "batboy" while covering the trip. It was Vic's first time riding the rails.[17] As the train pulled out of Oakland, he displayed a picture of his girlfriend, Betty Evans, in his berth. Among his other prized possessions in tow was a Camilli model Louisville Slugger. Vic spent much of his time sleeping and writing letters to Betty. When the train stopped in Ogden, Utah, Picetti received celebrity treatment. A local sportswriter, a politician, and a decorated veteran just off active duty all greeted him warmly. "If his physical makeup is a sample of his baseball ability, his name someday will be placed alongside that of Joe DiMaggio, Vince DiMaggio, Tony Lazzeri, Frankie Crosetti, and other famous Italian baseball performers," wrote the scribe.[18]

Picetti and Leiser decamped the train in Chicago for an overnight stay. Vic met with an acquaintance, Roger Brown, who would represent Minnesota in the All-American game. The pair had competed against one another the year before in the American Legion tournament in Montana. They became fast friends upon their reunion and arranged to be roommates for the remainder of the trip. *Esquire* provided the players with dinner and a penthouse suite in Chicago's Sherman Hotel.

After arriving in Manhattan, Picetti and his teammates checked into the New Yorker, a forty-two-story art deco hotel on Eighth Avenue between Thirty-Fourth and Thirty-Fifth Streets. The posh digs and complimentary meals made them feel like big leaguers. The boys were not completely on their own in the Big Apple; a high school principal from Buffalo served as a chaperone.

The teens engaged in several days of practices and sightseeing starting August 1. The West All-Americans practiced at the hallowed Polo Grounds, home ballpark of the New York Giants. The oddly configured stadium featured a horseshoe-shaped grandstand, ridiculously short left- and right-foot lines (279 and 257 feet, respectively), and an expansive center field that stretched to 483 feet from home plate. Vic and his teammates not only roamed the same field as legends Mel Ott and Carl Hubbell, but they also received coaching from them. Ott, still an active player-manager with the Giants, piloted the West team but was nursing an ankle injury, so Hubbell stepped in to lead the workouts. Besides Picetti and Brown, the West team included future Hall of Famer Richie Ashburn from Nebraska and eventual big league pitchers Erv Palica and Virgil Jester from Southern California and Colorado, respectively. Hubbell called the All-Americans "the greatest bunch of young ballplayers I've ever seen gathered in one ball yard."[19] After a morning practice, the boys enjoyed an afternoon boat tour around Manhattan and took in an evening show at Radio City Music Hall, which included a performance by the Rockettes.[20]

The next morning, the All-Americans played a practice game at the Polo Grounds. Picetti laced a double and impressed the legions of sportswriters observing the action, who agreed that he was destined to hit many more blasts in big-league ballparks before long. Vic spent the afternoon touring the Statue of Liberty, the landmark that greeted his parents when they arrived from Italy four decades earlier.[21]

Talent evaluators representing all sixteen major-league teams lingered in the New Yorker lobby and observed practices and games, hoping to someday land one of the talented teenagers. Picetti's name was at the top of every scout's list. In the eyes of Wish Egan, a recruiter for the Detroit Tigers, no player stood out above Vic.[22] Even among the best amateurs in the country, Picetti appeared poised and even-keeled.[23]

Picetti received a visit from Dodgers general manager Branch Rickey at his hotel and was among the players who dined with the Brooklyn executive on August 4.[24] After dinner, Picetti had the choice of attending a war bond drive boxing match at Madison Square Garden or the Dodgers–Braves game at Ebbets Field. He chose the ball game and got to meet Dodgers manager Leo Durocher, whose team was fighting to stay out of the National League cellar. "If any of you have not had enough work yet today, come on out and join us. We can use some help," he told the group of boys.[25] The Bums, as the Dodgers were known, claimed a rare victory that night. Two days later, many of the boys chose to stay inside because of a suffocating heat wave hitting the East Coast. Vic, however, did not pass up the opportunity to see a doubleheader between the Phillies and Giants at the Polo Grounds.

Picetti was experiencing things and meeting people he had only read about in newspapers and books or seen in movies, such as visiting the Empire State Building and having a lengthy conversation with Ott.[26] Undoubtedly one of his biggest thrills was meeting Babe Ruth, when the All-American boys appeared on the Bambino's weekly radio show.[27]

On the day of the All-American game, Vic gathered with his teammates in the hotel lobby in preparation for a jaunt north to the Polo Grounds. At the last minute, he realized he left some equipment in his room and went to fetch it. When he returned, everyone was gone. Vic wasn't sure which subway to take and ended up heading south toward Brooklyn. After changing trains four or five times, he finally made it to the Polo Grounds in Upper Manhattan just as the game was about to begin.[28]

Vic missed part of the pregame ceremony, which included performances by Abbott and Costello, Gene Krupa's orchestra, and Al Schacht—the first "Clown Prince of Baseball." Babe Ruth spoke and declared it didn't matter which team won so long as they played clean and hard.[29] The game was broadcast on the radio with Red Barber at the microphone. A vociferous crowd of 17,803 comprised of mostly youngsters made the noise of 50,000.

Vic and his teammates from the West donned newly issued gray uniforms with blue trim and blue hats. Picetti wore his baggy pants high and cinched at the waist. Ott's batting order included Picetti in the cleanup spot, playing first base. The East team was piloted by Connie Mack, the eighty-one-year-old owner and manager of the Philadelphia Athletics, who wore his usual suit and tie.

The West hitters had their hands full in the form of Billy Pierce, the starting pitcher for Mack's crew. Pierce earned the moniker "Mr. Zero" for the number of shutouts he threw on the sandlots of Detroit. The lefty's arsenal included an overpowering fastball and sharp breaking ball, which had already garnered him a contract with his hometown Tigers. Less than a year later, Pierce was in the big leagues. Twenty years later, he retired with 211 career wins and nearly two thousand strikeouts.

In the first inning, Picetti dug into the batter's box. Pierce was surely the toughest southpaw that he had ever faced. "The first curve he threw me looked high and inside until it came over the plate, and right there it stopped and dropped low and outside," described Picetti. "It fooled me so bad I just laughed."[30] Despite Pierce's elite repertoire, Vic made solid contact on one offering, redirecting the pitch into left-center field. The ball fell in between the converging outfielders as Vic reached second base with a double. Later in the game, he added a single, accounting for two of his team's six hits. The East defeated their West counterparts, 6–0. Pierce was named the game's Most Valuable Player, though Tiger scout Egan, unsolicited, told Bill Leiser that Vic was the most finished performer on the field.[31] Barber, calling the action over the airwaves, "went overboard for the Frisco kid."[32]

The best part of the trip for Vic was making friends with other ballplayers his age from around the country. By the end of the week, it seemed they had known each other for years. "I was very honored and very lucky to have been able to make this trip," Picetti wrote in article that he penned for the *San Francisco Chronicle*.[33]

Picetti was even more sought after on the heels of his showing at the *Esquire* All-American game. All sixteen major league teams plus the eight PCL clubs expressed interest. Joe Devine, the Northern California–based Yankees scout who signed Joe DiMaggio, had been watching Picetti for two years. "There isn't the slightest doubt in my mind that he will someday make good in the majors," opined Devine. "The kid is one of those naturals that pop up every so often."[34] Devine offered Picetti a contract, but it was fruitless; the youngster had already made up his mind. Before he left San Francisco for New York, Picetti verbally committed to playing for Camilli and the Oakland Oaks. The deal wasn't official, though, and Oaks' general manager Victor "Cookie" Devincenzi worried that a big league club could flatter Picetti in New York City and sway him to spurn Oakland for the major leagues.[35] The bright lights of Manhattan and higher bids from big league scouts did not dissuade the young phenom, however. A few days after returning home to San Francisco, Vic Sr. asked his son if he still wanted to sign with the Oaks. He said yes. "That's that, then," responded Vic Sr.[36]

Picetti signed with Oakland for a bonus of $2,500.[37] Vic Sr. believed he could have gotten $15,000 from the Yankees, Giants, or Red Sox.[38] The *San Francisco Chronicle* reported that Giants owner Horace Stoneham "had practically taken the rubber band off the bank roll" to sign him.[39] One report speculated that bids for Picetti from major league teams could have climbed to as high as $40,000.[40] The opportunity to play with his idol, just across the bay from home, was too enticing. Another factor weighed into the decision; Vic still had one more year of high school. By playing in Oakland, he could complete his studies during the day and play ball at night. Picetti planned to spend a year or two learning from Camilli and then jump to the majors. "Let it suffice to say both Vic and the Oakland people are well satisfied with the deal," Vic Sr. told one reporter.[41]

Pirates scout Hollis Thurston, who had tracked Picetti for two years, envied Camilli and the Oaks. "I had my eye on him for a long time and I sure wish we had him under lock and key," said Thurston. "He ought to become one of the best first basemen baseball has had."[42]

After finalizing his contract, Picetti boarded a train to meet up with his new team in Los Angeles, where they were set to take on the first-place Angels. Camilli moved himself to right field, allowing his prodigy to play first base. Picetti debuted on August 16 and made a pair of nifty plays with the glove to help secure a 1–0 victory for the Oaks.[43] The next day, he recorded his first professional base hit. Picetti played six games in the seven-game series, recording four hits in twenty at-bats. Other than his at-bat against southpaw Ray Prim, a former major leaguer with a tough curveball, Picetti never appeared overmatched.

"The boy's a cinch to wind up in the big time," said PCL president Clarence Rowland. "He's a natural ballplayer—and that goes for his bat as well as his glove. But what got me was his poise. Here he was, subbing for probably the greatest first baseman in organized ball, and you'd have thought it was nothing at all. He just went out there and played first base as if the job had been his for years. His footwork and stance at the plate couldn't be beat. He'll be heard from plenty."[44]

Besides his contract with the Oaks, Picetti also landed an endorsement deal with Hillerich & Bradsby Company—the manufacturer of Louisville Slugger bats. Picetti received lumber to his preferred specifications—thirty-five inches and thirty-three ounces—with his name engraved on the barrel.[45] It was the first contract provided by the bat company to a PCL player in three years, an indicator of how far his reputation had traveled.[46]

Picetti played fourteen games for the Oaks down the stretch. He managed ten hits in forty-eight at-bats and committed only one error in 110 chances at first base. In the fall, he returned to Mission High to complete his senior year and played in the semipro Alameda Winter League. New York Giants infielder Hal Luby saw him play and added to the consensus assessment that Picetti was a budding star. "[Steve] Legault struck him out once with a knuckleball but the next time up he hit the same pitch a country mile . . . what I like about Picetti is that he wasn't fooled by the same pitch twice," noted Luby.[47]

Major league teams continued efforts to buy the rights to Picetti from Oakland during the offseason. One club reportedly offered $50,000.[48] When spring rolled back around, however, Picetti still belonged to the Oaks and reported to spring training in Boyes Springs, California, forty-five miles north of San Francisco. Mission High's principal arranged for Picetti to attend morning classes in nearby Sonoma.[49] In the afternoons, he joined his Oaks teammates for workouts.

Vic Sr. paid his son a visit at spring camp. The elder Picetti had been experiencing a stomach ailment, but the pain had dissipated during his stay in Boyes Springs. "It's sure funny, I guess the air up there helps a lot," wrote Angela in a letter to Junior.[50] Camilli and Laws invited Vic Sr. to spend a week in camp with all expenses paid, but he declined. Back in San Francisco, his pain returned.

In the months since debuting with Oakland the previous summer, Picetti had improved significantly in the eyes of former Oaks outfielder Bill Rigney, whose Naval Air Station Alameda team faced the Oaks for a spring exhibition. The *San Francisco Chronicle* reported that Picetti was "hitting all line drives" and "pickling the horsehide."[51] Picetti's openness to coaching contributed to his rapid ascent. Oaks coach Lindo Storti was awed at how he could master a bit of instruction after being told only once.[52] Picetti gave credit to his mentor and manager in a letter to his parents: "I sure can hit a lot better since Camilli changed me around."[53]

As World War II entered its fourth year, teams in the major leagues and PCL were mostly comprised of players who received a medical discharge from the military or who had 4-F draft status because of some physical deficiency. Clubs filled out rosters with players who would normally have been considered too young, too old, or simply not talented enough for baseball's highest ranks. In 1944, for example, the Cincinnati Reds used fifteen-year-old pitcher Joe Nuxhall. A year later they signed forty-six-year-old Horace Lisenbee, who hadn't pitched in the big leagues in nine seasons. He saw action in thirty-one games and posted a 5.49 earned run average. The St. Louis Browns, winners of the American League pennant in 1944, employed one-armed outfielder Pete Gray in 1945. Bert Shepard, an army air force veteran who had his right leg amputated because of wounds sustained during a mission over Germany, pitched in a game for the Washington Senators on an artificial leg.

Picetti, seventeen, was at least a decade younger than most of his Oakland teammates. In the case of pitcher Sam Gibson, he was twenty-eight years younger. Nonetheless, Picetti was a great clubhouse fit and was well-liked by his more senior comrades. "He is quiet, well-mannered and has no touch of the swelled head that might be expected from a youngster who has received the high acclaim meted out to him this season," described Lee Dunbar of the *Oakland Tribune*.[54]

Camilli, still in the dual role of player-manager, handed over the starting first-base job to Picetti when the regular season began on March 31. Les Scarsella, a former Cincinnati Reds and Boston Braves first baseman and the defending PCL batting champion, was relegated to the outfield—much to his displeasure. Camilli smiled as his protégé rapped three doubles and drove in four runs in the first three games. His decision to bench himself in favor Picetti and other younger players drew criticism from some sportswriters, however. "This is my 20th season, and baseball isn't a game for old gaffers," said Camilli in defense. "If I thought I could play first base better than Vic Picetti, I'd bench him."[55] It was hard to argue with the skipper's assessment. Picetti hit .407 during a thirteen-game hitting streak to begin the season. He handled both fastballs and breaking pitches equally well and hit to all fields. The hot start only increased Vic's stock further, as evidenced by the Oaks' rumored asking price of $100,000—the equivalent of $1.6 million in 2023 dollars.[56]

Aside from Vic's trip to New York and his brief stint with the Oaks in 1944, he had not ventured far from home in his seventeen years. Living out of hotels on the road and being afforded a certain degree of independence was a newfound experience. "We can sleep as late as we want, and whenever we want," he wrote to his mother from San Diego in April 1945.[57]

On May 15, Picetti walloped his first professional home run in a victory against Sacramento. It was an impressive feat given the diminished quality of baseballs during wartime. Typically, a baseball's core is composed of cork and rubber wrapped in a multilayered rubber shell. Because of tank construction and Japan's control of Malaysia and the Dutch East Indies, rubber was in short supply, so the Spalding company had to come up with alternative materials that resulted in a deadened ball.[58]

With the substandard baseballs in use, only five Coast League players hit double-digit home run totals in 1945 despite playing schedules of 180 games or more. The Oaks as a team managed only forty-two round-trippers. "Balls got soft due to overuse," remembered Emil Mailho, an outfielder who hit only one home run for the San Francisco Seals that year. "Fans had to return any balls hit into the stands because of rationing. The ball we hit was like a rock because they couldn't use good rubber in them. It was all synthetic rubbers, so the ball didn't have any life to it."[59]

Dead baseballs aside, the Oaks' home ballpark was not particularly conducive to the long ball. The stadium, located in Emeryville, had outfield dimensions of 404 feet to center and 329 feet to left and right field. Wind gusts from the bay blew in from right field, sometimes causing fly balls that would normally travel to the outfield to land in the second baseman's glove. The park's infield light stands were in front of the dugouts and held large bucket lights that created shadows on the field. The scoreboard was located above the center-field wall, in the batter's eye. "When a guy would throw, the ball would come right out of the lights on the scoreboard, and when it was 2–2 or 3–2 on the batter, you had to bear down," recalled Oaks catcher Bill Raimondi.[60]

Picetti's professional baseball career could not have gotten off to a better start. He was thriving near his hometown as one of the youngest players in the PCL while learning the nuances of the game from his hero. But then came a devastating blow. His father died from cancer on May 28 at the age of forty-three. Junior, still only seventeen, had lost his biggest fan and suddenly became sole provider for his mother and two siblings. His love of the game was no longer the driving force behind his baseball pursuits; there were bills to pay.

Fifteen days after the death of Vic Sr., the Oaks abruptly fired Camilli. Though the Oaks were in third place and within striking distance of the first-place Portland Beavers, ownership was displeased with the thirty-eight-year-old player-manager for not putting himself in the lineup more often.[61] Camilli had taken only seventeen at-bats all season, yielding nearly all the first-base playing time to Picetti. "I cannot understand the two-faced attitude of the Oakland owners, who acted nice to my face but knifed me when my back was turned," Camilli told the press.[62] It is conceivable that Scarsella, perhaps still bitter about being moved off first base, may have undermined Camilli and lobbied ownership for his dismissal.[63] Days after his firing, Camilli signed with the Boston Red Sox to play what would be his final big-league games. Though Camilli and Picetti were now on opposite coasts, they kept in touch. Camilli penned a letter to Vic from Boston's Hotel Kenmore on July 12, 1945. He encouraged Vic to keep hustling and to not get discouraged if all of his hard-hit balls did not fall for base hits. Dolph also mentioned that he would rather be managing in Oakland but that he was getting along okay in Boston and had lost weight because of the sweltering heat out East.[64]

Camilli hit only .212 with two home runs in sixty-three games for the Red Sox as he finished out his distinguished career. Picetti, meanwhile, finished the season with a .281 batting average in 152 games for Oakland. One of the fastest players in the league, he led the Oaks in triples and stolen bases and tied for the team lead with eighty-six RBIs. "The kid has at last grown up," wrote the *Oakland Tribune*. "He now has the assurance a youngster needs to play Double-A or major-league ball."[65] It remained to be seen if the Oaks would cash out on their prized prospect during the offseason. If not, Picetti's immediate future would lie in the hands of the team's new manager: Casey Stengel.

4

AUTUMN 1945

No sport captured the attention of American sports fans in the 1920s more than baseball. Nearly every town in the country had some form of organized ball that served as a source of entertainment. If a talented player with big league potential sprouted up, he would be sold to the highest bidder. Maryland native Lefty Grove signed his first baseball contract with a Class D minor league team in Martinsburg, West Virginia, for $125 a month.[1] After he put together six impressive starts, Martinsburg turned around and sold him to the Baltimore Orioles, a Class AA minor league team. In five seasons with the Orioles, Grove posted a 108–36 record before the team sold him in 1925 to Connie Mack and the Philadelphia Athletics for $100,600.[2] Tony Lazzeri got his start in baseball playing for semipro teams in his hometown of San Francisco. In 1922, the eighteen-year-old infielder signed with the Pacific Coast League's Salt Lake City Bees, who three years later sold him to the New York Yankees for $50,000 and a pair of players.[3] Branch Rickey, general manager of the St. Louis Cardinals, realized his team could not outbid wealthier teams for players like Lazzeri and Grove, so he created his own farm system pipeline as a source of talent. Other major league teams followed suit, resulting in rapid expansion of minor leagues from coast to coast. By 1940, there were forty-four minor leagues in operation.[4] Some were affiliated with major league organizations, whereas others were independent ventures run by local entrepreneurs. Unaffiliated clubs would sign their own players or form working agreements with higher level teams to fill their rosters.

CHAPTER 4

Portland and Seattle were home to Pacific Coast League franchises, but in smaller Pacific Northwest cities, the Western International League (WIL) became the preeminent circuit when it formed in 1937. The WIL at various times included teams in Idaho, Oregon, Washington, and British Columbia. One of the league's charter members was Spokane, whose baseball roots dated back nearly a half-century. The city's first professional baseball game was played in May 1890 at Twickenham Park as part of the Pacific Northwest League, a four-team circuit that included the oddly named Seattle Hustlers, Tacoma Daisies, Portland Webfeet, and Spokane Bunch Grassers. The league was a brief success but folded after three seasons because of poor attendance. Attempts to revive the league in 1896 and 1898 were short-lived.

Spokane's next professional team debuted in 1901 and played its games at Natatorium Park, located at the end of a streetcar line near the Spokane River. A pine tree down the left-field line served as a foul pole. During its first two seasons, the team was informally known as the Blue Stockings and then the Smoke Eaters, but in its third year the *Spokesman-Review* held a contest to adopt an official team name. The winning suggestion, submitted by clothing salesman Arthur Pease, was Inlanders.[5] "This name appears to meet with general favor, though there is quite a following for Emperors and Indians," wrote the *Spokane Chronicle*.[6] A month later newspapers inexplicably began referring to the team as the Indians, and the name stuck. Beginning in 1905 the team played its home games at Recreation Park, a field so expansive that no player hit a home run until the Indians' third season there. The ballpark initially accommodated one thousand spectators, but because of baseball's growing popularity, every time the team went on the road, more seats were added until it held seven thousand.

In the 1910s, Spokane's rosters included players who would make their mark in baseball for very different reasons. Future Hall of Famers Stan Coveleski and George "High Pockets" Kelly and soon-to-be Yankees slugger Bob Meusel all suited up for the local nine. Another pair of Indians—Charles "Swede" Risberg and Shufflin' Phil Douglas—are two of only twenty-four men in major league history to receive a lifetime ban. Risberg received his punishment because of his involvement in the 1919 Black Sox scandal, whereas Douglas, a mercurial lefty who battled alcoholism, earned his banishment by offering to abscond from the 1922 New York Giants for money in order to hurt his team's pennant chances.[7]

Minor leagues across the country folded during World War I and the Great Depression. Spokane went sixteen years without a professional team until the WIL formed in 1937. For the first two seasons, the Spokane club went by the name Hawks. Then, local restaurateur Bill Ulrich, who co-owned the Recreation Room Tavern and Café with his brother, bought the franchise and wanted to rebrand the team. After gathering public opinion and months of deliberation, the name was changed to Indians. "Ulrich was influenced, no doubt, by the fact that Spokane itself is an Indian name, meaning "children of the sun," wrote the *Spokane Chronicle*.[8]

Besides the Indians, two other WIL teams—the Wenatchee Chiefs and Bellingham Chinooks—also had Native American–inspired nicknames. The Indians name had been under consideration when Spokane first entered the WIL in 1937, but the Seattle PCL franchise was called the Indians at the time, and so Hawks was chosen.[9] Owner Emil Sick had since rebranded Seattle's team as the Rainiers—the same name as his brewery. Under Ulrich's ownership, the highly successful 1940 and 1941 Spokane Indians set national attendance records among Class B leagues.[10]

During World War II, the number of minor leagues was reduced to just nine. The WIL became one of many circuits to suspend operations during wartime as 90 percent of professional ballplayers—more than five thousand in total—joined the war effort in some capacity. The atomic bombings of the Japanese cities of Hiroshima and Nagasaki in August 1945 effectively brought an end to the war. Within weeks, owners and officials of the disbanded minor leagues began to reorganize, including the WIL.

As the league prepared to restart following its wartime pause, Ulrich sold half of his shares in the team to Sam Collins, a native Montanan and cigar shop owner in Lewiston, Idaho. Two months later, Collins became sole owner when he bought out Ulrich's remaining shares and the Indians' home ballpark, Ferris Field, at a combined cost of $75,000.[11] Collins, who resembled a gaunt version of Branch Rickey, had a wooden leg because of a switch engine accident years earlier. He previously served as president of a Pioneer League franchise that played in Lewiston and Idaho Falls before the war.

In the fall of 1945, WIL officials gathered in Tacoma, Washington, to solidify plans to resume play the following spring. Attendees included league president Robert Abel, executives from four holdover franchises (Spokane, Tacoma, Vancouver, and Salem), and representatives from the

Pacific Coast League and major league baseball. Former big leaguers George Sisler and Ken Penner, scouts for the Dodgers and Cardinals, respectively, sought to secure affiliations for their organizations. The board discussed player salaries, agreeing to a cap of $3,000 per month, and debated whether to add two or four more teams to the league.[12] Bids from several potential members were considered, including applications from Victoria, Sacramento, Bremerton, Wenatchee, Pasco-Kennewick, and Yakima. The board agreed to admit Victoria, but competition among the other cities was so fierce that the board punted the issue. At subsequent meetings, league officials voted to admit Yakima, Wenatchee, and Bremerton, bringing the total number of teams to eight.

The reorganization of the WIL made headlines in the Pacific Northwest, but a story with broader ramifications was developing on the East Coast. Since the end of the war, calls to integrate the major leagues had grown louder. The Holocaust had opened America's eyes to the pernicious dangers of discrimination and provided fuel to address prejudice and racism in America. The contributions of African Americans during the war furthered the cause. Rickey, now the general manager of the Brooklyn Dodgers, assessed that it was an opportune time to end baseball's color barrier. On October 23, he signed Jackie Robinson to a minor league contract with the Dodgers' top farm team, the Montreal Royals. Not everyone embraced baseball's desegregation. In a secret vote after Robinson's signing, fifteen out of the sixteen major league owners chose against allowing Black players into the big leagues. The Dodgers cast the lone dissenting vote. After meeting with Rickey, however, baseball's new commissioner, Albert "Happy" Chandler, the former governor of Kentucky, vowed to approve the signing.

As the leaves turned and temperatures cooled in Spokane, Collins sought to form working agreements with a Coast League team or two in order to ensure a source of talent for the upcoming season. He spent most of October in California meeting with officials from five PCL clubs but returned home without a formal pact. Collins next turned his attention to hiring a manager, settling on Glenn Wright, a native Missourian who came to baseball prominence in the 1920s as a member of the Pittsburgh Pirates. Wright hit .294 in eleven big league seasons, won a World Series title with the Bucs in 1925, and once turned an unassisted triple play—one of the rarest of all baseball feats.[13] After Wright's playing career, he managed the Wenatchee Chiefs for three seasons before landing a coaching position with the PCL's Hollywood Stars. Wright's habit of showing up late resulted in his dismissal during his second season on the job. During the war, he spent three years in the navy, serving as a quartermaster instructor at Camp Farragut, Idaho.

In December 1945, Collins and Wright traveled to Columbus, Ohio, for the national minor league meetings. There, Collins solved the conundrum of filling his roster by securing working agreements with the New York Yankees and two PCL teams—the Oakland Oaks and San Diego Padres. The latter two clubs agreed to send a combined thirteen players, and Yankees farm director George Weiss promised seven or eight. Collins happily maintained the status of an independent organization with informal ties to multiple teams rather than relying on a single team to send players.[14]

Collins's offseason planning was interrupted by a hospitalization and undisclosed surgery in January.[15] He returned to work a few weeks later and hired former Spokane Indians player Dwight Aden to serve as his team's business manager. Before the war, Aden patrolled center field for Spokane and hit .310 in five seasons. Since his discharge from the navy, he had gone into the insurance business.[16] In addition to Aden, Collins also employed his own daughter, Joyce, as team secretary.

Collins arranged a three-week spring training for the Indians in Marysville, California. The location offered the prospect of decent April weather and proximity to Coast League and semipro teams for practice games. In the weeks leading up to camp, Wright traveled to California to scout the Oaks and Padres at their respective spring training sites. Collins and Aden, meanwhile, worked on independently securing their own players. One of the first to sign was thirty-two-year-old outfielder Levi McCormack, one of Spokane's most beloved players and a former teammate of Aden.

Levi Warren McCormack, born on June 11, 1913, in Lapwai, Idaho, was a member of the Nez Perce Tribe. He was a multisport star in his prep days at Lapwai High School and then played collegiate football, basketball, and baseball at Washington State. Because of his heritage and athletic feats, he drew comparisons to Jim Thorpe.[17] McCormack, six-feet-one with broad shoulders and blazing foot speed, left college in 1936 to sign with the Seattle Indians of the PCL. He played in a handful of games that summer and then served as a part-time outfielder the next two seasons. He performed well when given the opportunity, but he had a hard time cracking a lineup that included older, more established teammates and fellow prospect Edo Vanni. After the 1938 season, the Seattle franchise, then known as the Rainiers, optioned McCormack to the Spokane Indians.

McCormack's all-out hustle, productive bat, and enthusiasm with which he signed autographs for kids made him a fan favorite in Spokane. "If he got on first and someone moved him to third, he would throw out his chest and the ladies would just howl," recalled Aden.[18] McCormack was affectionately nicknamed "Chief," a moniker that was all too often given to Native Americans in the early twentieth century. In his case, however, the title was fitting, given that he was the son of an actual Nez Perce chief. In 1940, McCormack hit .327, scored 130 runs, and accumulated 108 RBIs for the first-place Indians, who fell to the Tacoma Tigers in the league playoffs. He performed even better in 1941, hitting .338 with a .485 on-base percentage while propelling Spokane to its first league title.

After three standout seasons, the Indians sold McCormack to the Coast League's Portland Beavers for $1,500.[19] Before he could suit up in Portland flannels, McCormack enlisted in the navy, where he played ball for the highly successful Naval Air Station Seattle Flyers. The Flyers, who later relocated to Pasco, Washington, dominated service and pro teams alike, racking up a 62–7 record over the course of two years.[20] McCormack then spent nine months in the South Pacific, including stints in the Marianas, Guam, and Saipan.[21] After his military discharge, McCormack hoped to link up with a PCL team, but the league had no vacancies because of players returning from the war, so he gladly agreed to return to Spokane.

As spring training approached, Collins and Aden also signed George Lyden, a right-hander who had pitched briefly for the Indians before the war. Lyden, like McCormack, came from the Idaho panhandle, the fifth of six children born to Fred and Bethel (née May) Lyden. Fred worked as a teamster, manning a horse-drawn combine on farms throughout Idaho. Money was scarce, so George and his three brothers worked odd jobs for nickels and dimes. The Lyden boys spent weekends playing baseball for semipro clubs or any team that needed an extra player. George's older brother, Jim, played for the Spokane Hawks in 1937.

George first made a name for himself in baseball as an eighteen-year-old pitching in a Kansas semipro tournament. As a result of his stellar performance, the Spokane Indians inked him to a contract. Just before the 1942 season, he married Elizabeth "Betty" Donahoe. They welcomed their first son, Allen, nine months later. Lyden pitched in six games for the 1942 Indians and struggled with his control, issuing twenty-six walks in forty-two innings.

Lyden enlisted in the navy and began active duty in August 1942. While stationed in Memphis, Tennessee, he worked on his pitching with a semipro team and played basketball for a military squad. During his time in the navy, he and Betty welcomed a second son named Larry. Money was a constant worry for George, whose primary concern was providing for Betty and their two boys. Professional baseball had the potential to provide a nice income if he could climb the ladder to the PCL or major leagues. Instead, it would take his life.

5

SPRING TRAINING 1946

The Sonoma Mission Inn, built in 1927 on the site of the old Boyes Hot Springs Resort in California's picturesque Sonoma Valley, had the feel of a charming European estate. The mission-style building had an arcaded entrance, red-tiled floors, and bell towers. Its amenities included a glass-enclosed swimming pool and an eighteen-hole golf course. The luxury hotel went out of business during the Great Depression and was leased by the navy during World War II to serve as a rest and recuperation center for sailors and marines on leave from the Pacific theater. In February and March 1946, it provided spring training housing for the Oakland Oaks baseball club.

Vic Picetti was one of more than fifty ballplayers—many of them recently discharged servicemen—who came to Oaks camp hoping to crack Casey Stengel's roster. The new skipper had been lured to Oakland from his hometown of Kansas City, where he had been managing the Yankees' top farm team. The Oaks paid him $12,000 and gave him full autonomy in roster decisions.[1] Casey and his wife, Edna, made their offseason home in the Los Angeles suburb of Glendale, which added to the appeal of managing in the Pacific Coast League (PCL). Oaks executives Brick Laws and Cookie Devincenzi counted on Stengel's name recognition and larger-than-life personality to attract fans to the ballpark. Stengel also brought connections from managing the Brooklyn Dodgers and Boston Braves, which Oaks brass hoped could attract big league talent. It helped that the PCL, which operated independently, drew more fans than some major league teams and in some cases paid better. For many players living on the West Coast, it was as desirable as the big leagues.

During the Oaks' first practice, Stengel focused his attention on Picetti, who reported to camp with fifteen pounds of added muscle after spending the winter packing bricks for a mason.[2] Though he impressed Stengel that day, the eighteen-year-old first baseman faced a difficult path to a starting job with the Oaks, whose roster was now full of more established players in their late twenties and early thirties. Picetti's primary competition at the first sack was Les Scarsella, who was two years removed from the PCL batting title and Most Valuable Player Award. Scarsella, a natural first baseman, had been relegated to the outfield by Dolph Camilli in 1945 so Picetti could play first base. But Scarsella now had the advantage of having played first base for Stengel in Boston. Plus, the Old Perfessor had a strong preference for veteran players. Returning Scarsella to the outer pasture was not an ideal option; the Oaks' crowded outfield group included veterans Hersh Martin, Charlie Metro, Brooks Holder, and Wally Westlake, not to mention several promising prospects.

The Oaks played their first spring exhibition against a team organized by former New York Giants infielder Hal Luby, whose squad included a couple of big leaguers named Eddie—Lake and Joost. The game took place in teeth-chattering cold and went fifteen innings. Picetti played the entire contest and registered a pair of safeties in eight at-bats. The Oaks' offense was led by Bob Paterson, who entered the game in the sixth inning and proceeded to triple, double, and then single home the winning run. Paterson opened the eyes of his manager. "He must be reckoned as a candidate for one of those outfield jobs," remarked Stengel.[3]

Robert Duncan Paterson was born on April 16, 1924, in San Francisco to James and Clara (née Carr) Paterson, second-generation Irish Americans who stood a shade above and below five feet tall, respectively. James worked as a pattern maker at Bethlehem Steel and played music on the side. Despite his genetics, Bob grew to be six-feet-four. Both he and his older sister, Dorothy, towered over their parents in photos. Bob had light brown hair, deep-set blue eyes, a long neck, and a prominent chin. One sportswriter likened him to a young Lou Gehrig.[4] The Patersons lived in a turn-of-the-century three-story Victorian in San Francisco's Eureka Valley neighborhood. Bob starred in baseball at Mission High School three years ahead of Vic Picetti and, like Vic, played American Legion ball for Rincon Hill. He signed with the Oakland Oaks at age seventeen for a salary of $100 per month.[5]

In 1942, the Oaks farmed Paterson out to the Idaho Falls Russets in the Pioneer League—the same circuit as Jack Lohrke's Twin Falls Cowboys. Paterson and Lohrke, both eighteen, were among the youngest players in the league. Like most novices in professional baseball, Paterson learned to navigate the ups and downs in a sport where the best hitters fail seven out of ten times. At 2:00 a.m. on July 18, hours after the Russets defeated the Salt Lake City Bees, 7–5, in front of a sparse home crowd of 474, Bob laid in bed and listened to the radio.[6] As he thought of his family back home in San Francisco, he decided to get up and write a letter:

> Dear Folks,
>
> Received your letter upon our return from Twin Falls where we didn't fair out very good. We lost three games, and I got only one hit in all of them. We played Salt Lake tonight and won 7 to 5. I got two hits and drove in the first two runs. It seems that whenever I start hitting good, I get careless and before I know it, I'm in a slump. It gets so bad sometimes that I wish I had never played baseball but then I make up my mind to do good and I do better. Experience is the main thing in baseball. In the last four series I have caught the third baseman napping and have beat out four sneak bunts. If you are heads-up and hustle you can do good.
>
> I intend to make you all proud of me when I get back, even if I shouldn't hit .300, as long as I have a good reputation and the pitchers consider me dangerous, I'll be satisfied. Someday everyone will know me, and you will be proud of me. I have made up my mind to be one of the best or else drop the game.[7]

Bob was open and honest with his family. He went on to write about a "swell" red-headed girl he had been seeing and admitted that he often enjoyed a beer after games.

At the end of July, Paterson led Idaho Falls with a .305 batting average—69 points higher than the team mark.[8] According to his manager, erstwhile Chicago White Sox and PCL hurler Lou Garland, scouts considered him the best prospect in the league. A St. Louis Cardinals talent hawk wanted to buy his contract from the Russets, but the Oaks owned his rights.[9]

Oaks general manager Cookie Devincenzi caught wind of Paterson's stellar play and summoned him to Oakland in August. A telegram sent to Garland said, "Due to injuries and enlistments, we would like to recall Paterson if you can spare him."[10] Garland approached Paterson with the opportunity, and they talked it over during batting practice. Paterson was conflicted. In his estimation, he needed more experience and thought his throwing arm wasn't as strong as it needed to be at that moment, but there was no guarantee that he would get another shot in the PCL. Based on their conversation, Garland sent a telegram back to Oakland indicating Paterson could not help them because of his arm.

After Paterson talked it over with teammates, who told him he should have gone to Oakland, he second-guessed his decision and wondered if he had squandered his one big chance. The situation caused him many sleepless nights and he admittedly failed to show his usual all-out hustle for several games.

"I didn't care if I struck out or not," Paterson wrote in a letter to his family. "I know I will get over it, but it is going to be tough because I will always think that I had a chance and muffed it because I was too hasty."[11]

Paterson came to the realization that he needed to put the matter behind him and put forth his best effort. As the season wound down, he put together a nineteen-for-forty stretch and ended the campaign with a team-leading .316 batting average.

Paterson enlisted in the US Coast Guard during the war and honed his baseball skills for a service team called the Port Battalion Surf Riders. During his three years protecting the California coastline, he married the former Dorothy Saylor and measured himself against proven baseball stars in the highly competitive All-Service League, which played games on Sundays between April and August and included the likes of former or future big leaguers Charlie Gehringer, Cookie Lavagetto, Bill Rigney, Wally Judnich, Charlie Silvera, Wally Westlake, Bill Wight, and Ferris Fain. When a pair of all-star teams were selected for a benefit game, Paterson was tabbed to play left field for the all-navy squad managed by Gehringer, a Hall of Fame second baseman from the Detroit Tigers.[12]

One of Bob's highlights the following summer came on August 6, 1944, against a team of fighter pilot cadets from St. Mary's Pre-Flight. In front of three thousand spectators at Seals Stadium, he belted a home run over the left-field fence off of Washington Senators pitcher Ray Scarborough.[13] The Surf Riders went on to defeat Livermore Naval Air Station in a three-game playoff to capture the league title. At the conclusion of the season, Paterson was chosen as the center fielder for the league's all-star nine.[14]

Paterson, a month shy of his twenty-third birthday, brimmed with confidence at his first spring training since the war. On a publicity questionnaire, he wrote that his goal was to "be the best there ever was."[15] The way he was hitting balls a country mile in batting practice and now dazzling in his first exhibition with the Oaks, anything seemed possible. "There's a boy who has plenty of what it takes," said Yankees scout Joe Devine after Paterson's three-hit performance. "He should go places in baseball. Sure, I'm interested in him. What scout wouldn't be."[16]

Chris Hartje, competing at catcher for the Oaks, had played for a coast guard outfit called the Sea Lions, one of the Surf Riders' competitors in the ten-team service league. Though he came with some big league experience, Hartje was a long shot to make Stengel's roster. Oakland had three returning catchers in the fold, including longtime backstop Billy Raimondi and former Yankee Eddie Kearse. Hartje, almost thirty-one years old and seven years removed from his cup of coffee with the Brooklyn Dodgers, made his case in an intrasquad game on March 7 by knocking a triple and two doubles.[17] His trio of extra-base hits would not be enough to unseat his competition, however. The Oaks released Hartje eight days later. He resurfaced three months later in Spokane.

Bob Kinnaman, a pitcher contending for a spot on Stengel's staff, furthered his cause with five scoreless innings against an army team on a brisk afternoon in mid-March.[18] An outgoing twenty-eight-year-old righty, Kinnaman was attempting to resurrect a baseball career after nearly four years in the military. He hailed from rural southwest Washington State, where he grew up playing sports and enjoying the great outdoors. While hunting, he developed skills that would later help him achieve elite status in military shooting drills. The former Washington State Cougar signed his first professional contract with the Twin Falls Cowboys of the Pioneer League in 1939.[19] The next year, he moved up a level to the Spokane Indians, where he won six games—one of which was a seven-inning no-hitter in the second game of a doubleheader versus Salem. Kinnaman took a line drive to the face off the bat of Nanny Fernandez during the 1940 season that knocked out eight teeth. The ball was hit so hard that his teammates turned a double play off the carom.[20]

Kinnaman returned to Spokane in 1941, winning twenty-two games with a sparkling 2.85 earned run average. He hoped his strong showing would catapult him to a higher league. "It'd be pretty nice to get peddled upstream, to see if you've really got it on the ball to earn the kind of money they'll pay up there," Kinnaman told the *Spokane Chronicle* at the end of that season.[21] His goal seemed to become a reality when the Portland Beavers bought his contract from Spokane for $5,000—a hefty price for a Class B player.[22] The Japanese bombed Pearl Harbor and Germany declared war on the United States that same month, however, and Kinnaman joined the war effort before ever throwing a pitch for Portland. As a result, his contract was voided and reverted to Spokane. The navy rejected Kinnaman because of his missing teeth, so he instead joined the army.[23] He became a member of the 333rd Engineer Company at Camp Claiborne, Louisiana, where he pitched for a service team.[24] He worked on construction projects at several stateside military bases before the army sent him to the European theater, where he achieved a rank of first sergeant. The Spokane Indians, like the majority of minor league teams, ceased operations during the war, so Kinnaman became a free agent upon his return to civilian life. Both major and minor league scouts showed interest in signing him before he agreed to terms with Oakland.

Glenn Wright observed the Oaks in Boyes Springs in late March, sizing up players who would be optioned to his Spokane club in the coming days. When the Oaks decamped, Picetti and Kinnaman were among the thirty players Stengel kept on his expanded roster to start the season. Fourteen others were dispersed to three teams in the Western International League. Bob Paterson and Pete Barisoff were among those sent to the Spokane Indians, who opened their spring camp one hundred miles away on April Fool's Day.

The Indians trained in Marysville, a small town in the Sacramento Valley born out of the Gold Rush a century earlier. A busload of ten players, including Levi McCormack, George Lyden, free agent signee Mel Cole, and several amateur hopefuls made the long journey from Spokane. Others, like

Jack Lohrke and Freddie Martinez of the Padres, arrived from Southern California. Rain-soaked grounds limited the team to handshakes and stretching on the first day of camp. The clouds parted and the ballfields dried over subsequent days, allowing the dozens of players in camp to practice hitting and fielding.

The power of Bob James was the talk of Marysville early on. The left-handed swinger blasted two home runs over the deep right-field fence in his first round of batting practice. James, a twenty-five-year-old Arizonan, had broad shoulders and a thick neck. His mother, a former schoolteacher, and father, a cotton farmer and rancher, met in Arkansas and moved west in 1918. Bob, the middle of three children, grew to be an outstanding athlete and popular student leader at Tempe High School. In addition to being an excellent baseball player, he served as class president for three years and captained the football team as an all-state fullback.[25] James drew interest from Boston Red Sox and Cincinnati Reds scouts during his senior year but elected to enroll at Santa Clara University, where he was a three-sport letterman.[26] The New York Yankees enticed him to sign after his freshman year and sent him to Idaho Falls in the summer of 1941—a year before Paterson was there. James batted .299 for the Russets, hit a team-high nine home runs, and led the Pioneer League with twenty-one outfield assists.[27] He put baseball aside during the war to perform agricultural work.[28] He enlisted in the navy in 1944 and received a farmworker's discharge the following year. James was now attempting a return to organized baseball after four years away from the game.

On April 6 and 7, the Indians played their first exhibition games and suffered a pair of losses to the Wenatchee Chiefs. Spokane's pitching left something to be desired, but Lohrke acquitted himself well at the plate and outfielders McCormack, Paterson, and James played solid defense. Paterson and James continued to impress in a pair of victories versus the Class C Stockton Ports on April 13 and 14. James peppered the ball three times and drove in five of the Indians' seven runs in the first game. His baserunning, on the other hand, was as rusty as an old Model T. In one instance, he clubbed the ball off the right-field wall and then slid headfirst into second base, only to find that it was already occupied by Paterson. In his next at-bat, James cranked one off the center-field fence, then was thrown out by ten feet trying to stretch a double into a triple. "I guess I can find ways of stopping him at second if he will just continue to powder that ball against the outfield fences," said Wright.[29] Paterson went five for eight and demonstrated fine abilities as a ball hawk in the outfield. One reporter declared that he was "a half step away from playing in the Coast League."[30]

After two weeks of practices and games, many of the unproven arms in camp had failed to impress Wright. The only pitchers who had secured their place on the roster were Barisoff and Dick Powers, a twenty-nine-year-old right-hander who had pitched in relief for Sacramento in the PCL the previous two seasons. Powers, an Ohio native, had jumped at the chance to become a starter with Spokane. In the third and final week of camp before heading north, the Indians received additional pitching help from the Padres, who sent pitchers Darwin "Gus" Hallbourg and Milt Cadinha. Unlike many of Wright's other pitching options, Hallbourg and Cadinha had experienced success pitching in the minor leagues before the war. Hallbourg, a native Massachusettsan, won forty-five games in three years of Class C and D ball before serving in the navy. Cadinha compiled twenty-six wins for the Tacoma Tigers before his stint in the army, which included service in the European and Pacific theaters.

With the pitching staff bolstered and spring training concluded, the Indians made the arduous two-day bus trek to Spokane. At the same time, Stengel cut down his roster and sent two more players packing to Spokane: Kinnaman and Picetti. Neither had played much for Oakland in the early going; Kinnaman had made just two relief appearances and Picetti managed just one hit in his thirteen at-bats. Stengel held Picetti in high regard but decided it was better to farm him out so he could play regularly.

On April 25, Picetti disembarked from a train in balmy Spokane, where temperatures topped 80 degrees. He sent his mother a Western Union telegram to let her know that he arrived safely then checked into the Halliday Hotel. Though it was much smaller than Picetti's bustling hometown of San Francisco, Spokane had—in a relatively short time—grown by leaps and bounds from its humble beginnings.

Prior to the nineteenth century, Indigenous peoples—including the Spokane, Coeur d'Alene, Yakama, Palouse, Walla Walla, and Nez Perce tribes—inhabited the Inland Northwest for thousands of years. The Spokane band of natives inhabited roughly three million acres in what is now northeastern

Washington State along the Spokane and Columbia Rivers.[31] Lewis and Clark explored southeastern Washington Territory via the Snake River in 1805, and European fur traders, explorers, and entrepreneurs slowly began arriving to the region. The Indigenous peoples at first welcomed the traders and the opportunity to acquire goods, but White settlers overran the region in the decades that followed.[32] In the 1850s, the United States government began surveying land in Washington Territory to build the Northern Pacific Railroad. With settlers encroaching and no formal treaty in place, tensions grew to the point of an armed conflict in 1858 known as the Spokane-Coeur d'Alene Indian War. The Indigenous tribes, including the Spokane, were forced onto reservations. The government formally recognized the Spokane Indian Reservation, an area of more than 154,000 acres, in 1881.[33]

The city of Spokane, named after the native tribe, was established on the banks of the Spokane River adjacent to a series of low falls. It flourished in the late nineteenth century because of the region's logging and mining industries and westward expansion of transcontinental railroads. As the population grew from 350 in 1880 to 104,402 in 1910, Spokane rapidly evolved into the inland's commercial center.[34] The downtown area was replete with brick hotels, clothiers, jewelers, taverns, and theaters. The Indians' home park, Ferris Field, stood a few miles east of downtown.

Picetti joined his new teammates at the ballpark and received his uniform from trainer John "Dutch" Anderson, a fellow San Franciscan and Mission High alum. Anderson worked as a pressman back in California, and his gig as the Indians' athletic trainer served as a second job and a way to be involved in the game he loved. Picetti received white sanitary socks, black stirrups, white pants, and a black belt. The jerseys were white with black trim, with *Spokane* written across the chest in black lettering. The caps were black with a white *S*. Picetti would don the threads the following night in the season opener.

Baseball was returning to Spokane after three long years. Everything seemed to be going swimmingly. That is, until less than twenty-four hours before the first pitch of the season, when Sam Collins abruptly fired manager Glenn Wright.

6

BASEBALL RESUMES IN SPOKANE

I know I'm a lucky fellow to get this job and I want the people to know I'll do my best and so will the players. If I didn't think I could handle the job, I wouldn't have accepted it. The boys are going to hustle and we're going to win.

—Mel Cole[1]

Cole's optimistic words were spoken hours before the Spokane Indians' home opener. Originally slated to be the team's starting catcher, he would now both play and manage. In many ways, life had prepared Cole for the challenge. Before the war, he spent five seasons playing for six different teams in the New York Yankees' farm system. In the navy, he played ball at the Sand Point Naval Training Station with Levi McCormack before sailing to the South Pacific on the USS *Hammondsport* in October 1943.[2] Cole served eighteen months in the Asian theater, including Guadalcanal, as an aviation machinist's mate first class.[3] While on active duty, he also gained experience managing a service team. So when Sam Collins found himself in need of a new manager on the eve of opening day, Cole seemed like the best choice.

Melvin Cole, born in Stockton, California, was one of five children reared by railroad conductor Chester Cole and his wife, Irene. A cousin of big league catchers Wally and Bobby Schang, Mel played shortstop in his amateur days and signed with the Yankees out of Sacramento High

School in 1937.[4] The Yankees assigned him to a Class D team in El Paso, Texas, where he broke a league record with a twenty-six game hitting streak and made the league's All-Star team.[5] During the next two seasons, Cole advanced up the Yankees' chain to Joplin, Missouri, and then Wenatchee, where he played for manager Glenn Wright—the man he would replace seven years later. Cole missed time in 1939 due to a beaning and then suffered through an illness before being sent down a rung to Class C Lewiston, Idaho. He then bounced around among Wenatchee, Idaho Falls, and Tacoma during the next two seasons. By then, he developed into a versatile utilityman who could fill in anywhere on the diamond.

Cole had brown hair, hazel eyes, and a youthful face. As a teenager, he was described as appearing anemic, but he filled out his five-feet-eleven frame during his forty-four months of wartime service in the navy.[6] Cole still aimed to make a living in baseball on his return to civilian life. When he completed a publicity questionnaire for the American Baseball Bureau in early 1946, he subtracted two years from his age, likely to make himself more appealing as a prospect.[7] Now he would have a chance to build his resume in pro ball as a manager.

Collins kept his reasons for firing Wright vague in the press, saying the decision was "due to ill health and for the good of baseball in Spokane."[8] It would eventually come to light that Wright went on a bender in the days leading up to the start of the season. "Glenn was a terrific guy," recalled Gus Hallbourg years later. "But he was drunk from the time we left Marysville to when we got back to Spokane."[9] Collins, recovering from a second surgery in four months, wasn't in the mood to put up with such shenanigans. Wright later found sobriety through Alcoholics Anonymous.[10]

Ferris Field, nestled on the western edge of the former Spokane Interstate Fairgrounds, was named after George Ferris, an attorney and former Spokane player who had helped secure funding to build the ballpark in 1936. It had a single tiered wooden grandstand, which housed locker rooms and had a roof to shield patrons from the elements. Down the left- and right-field lines were sets of bleachers. The Northern Pacific and Union Pacific Railroad tracks ran parallel to the first- and third-base lines and converged behind the grandstand. Advertisements for Schick Injector Razors, Triple XXX Barrel Diner ("Quick service in your car, Juicy Pig Bar-B-Q Sandwiches!"), and

Oscar Levitch's jewelry store were plastered on the outfield wall. The property was shared with a thoroughbred racetrack called Playfair Race Course, which was located beyond the outfield wall. A general admission ticket cost 80 cents; bleacher seats went for a half-dollar.

A cold front plummeted the mercury 30 degrees for the season opener on the evening of April 26. The toasty weather of the previous day had been only a tease; summer was still many weeks away. The smell of hot dogs and popcorn permeated the air as a crowd of 3,681 filed in. In the tiny, elevated press box, a hot plate kept coffee warm for the sportswriters.

The Indians' first opponent was the Vancouver Capilanos, a team piloted by longtime big-league pitcher Sylvester Johnson. Cole wrote out a lineup of Dunn (SS), Picetti (1B), Paterson (CF), Lohrke (3B), McCormack (LF), Risk (RF), Dunham (2B), Cole (C), and Cadinha (P). Bob James, slotted to be the Indians' starting right fielder, was not yet eligible to play because his option papers had not arrived. The game began after a ceremonial first pitch by Spokane mayor Arthur Meehan, who threw a one-hopper to Governor Monrad Wallgren.

Fourteen-year-old Kenny Benshoof made his debut that night as Spokane's batboy. The local youngster, who once caddied for Bing Crosby, took the initiative to call Sam Collins before the season to ask if the team needed a batboy. "I loved playing ball," remembered Benshoof decades later. "I thought, gee, this would be a great job. Not so much to make money—just something I wanted to do."[11] Benshoof received $1 per game and supplemented his income by bringing players bottles of Coke and pouches of chewing tobacco from the concession stand during the game for a marked-up price.

The Indians came out swinging in the bottom of the first inning against Vancouver starter Alex Palica, whose brother Erv played with Vic Picetti at the *Esquire* All-American game. Dunn reached on an error to lead off the game, then advanced to third on Picetti's single. Paterson followed with a two-run double and then scored on a double steal. The three-run lead was more than enough for Cadinha, who alternated between fastballs and curves to author a two-hit, thirteen-strikeout shutout. The crowd was entertained by the Indians' 5–0 victory as well as a stray dog that ran on the field midgame. The Vancouver outfielders made feeble attempts to catch the nimble canine before it finally left of its own volition.[12] The Indians proceeded to take two of the next three from the Capilanos behind strong pitching efforts by Hallbourg and Powers. Picetti banged out six hits in the four-game series.

Just as the Indians prepared to depart for their first road trip of the season, starting second baseman Will Dunham abruptly quit the team to pursue a business venture in Walla Walla. He cited the lack of available accommodations in Spokane as a factor in his decision.[13] A housing shortage was causing havoc from coast to coast, Spokane included. The problem was exacerbated by landlords and real estate agents who inflated prices. In some instances, prospective renters became so desperate they offered up their cars in exchange for a place to live. The issue even extended to the major leagues. Several members of the Washington Senators spent the first week of the season living in the clubhouse, and the Chicago White Sox advertised season tickets for anyone who assisted the team's players in finding housing.[14] Dunham's sudden departure meant Freddie Martinez would slot in at the keystone.

The Indians' next opponent was the Salem Senators. The 420-mile bus ride to the western Oregon town took sixteen tedious hours. "We go all over in a lousy bus, sure is miserable," wrote Picetti from the Hotel Marion in Salem.[15] When Bill Ulrich owned the team, the Indians had their own bus, but now they chartered coaches that had been neglected during the war. The Senators' lineup, which included future big league manager Frank Lucchesi and eventual Detroit Tiger Sam Vico, roughed up Spokane pitching, scoring fifty-five runs over seven games—an average of nearly eight runs per game. Spokane's offense scored twenty-five runs in the first four contests, then mustered only four in the final three. The result was a series sweep for the Senators, who remained undefeated through eleven games. The Indians cut four pitchers after the shellacking, lowering their roster to twenty-three players. They had until June 15 to get to the league limit of seventeen.

Despite their eight-game losing streak, the Indians remained upbeat as they returned home for another series versus Vancouver at Ferris Field on May 8. The Indians routed the Capilanos, 11–0, behind a one-hitter by Cadinha in the series opener. James and Martinez led the offensive attack with three hits apiece. Spokane won both ends of doubleheader the following day to complete a three-game sweep.

Spokane next hosted the Senators for four games with an opportunity to avenge the previous week's debacle in Salem. The Senators had finally lost to Wenatchee the day before, after reeling off thirteen straight to start the season. In the first game, six Salem errors aided Spokane in an 8–5 victory. The next night, Bob Kinnaman outpitched former Philadelphia Athletics righty Steve Gerkin in another Indians triumph that evened Spokane's record at 8–8. Each team claimed a victory in a series-concluding Sunday doubleheader. Cadinha, the winning pitcher in the nightcap, improved to 3–0 and had racked up thirty-three strikeouts in thirty-six innings.[16]

Through the Indians' first eighteen games, George Risk had emerged to lead the team in hitting with a .388 average.[17] Originally projected as a utilityman to start the season, he hit well while filling in for Bob James in the opening series and had forced his way into the lineup as the Indians' starting shortstop.

Risk grew up in Skamokawa, a small village on the Columbia River in southwest Washington. Blue-eyed and brown-haired, with a squinting smile and average build, Risk was a four-year baseball letterman and quarterback at Pacific University before entering the army at Fort Lewis in 1942, the same year he married Marjorie Sigler. Risk spent the war years stationed in Kearns, Utah, where he played on the Army Air Forces Overseas Replacement Training Center team called the Eagles. His .382 batting average in 1944 led a team that included prominent minor league slugger Jack Graham and former Yankee Johnny Sturm.[18] Commanding officers at Kearns and other Utah military bases forbade soldiers from participating in semipro leagues, so several servicemen used aliases to toil on the sandlots. Risk played under the pseudonym Al Seeglar.[19] After his discharge from the army, Risk was passed around like a collection plate on Sunday. He signed with the New York Yankees, who farmed him out to the Kansas City Blues, who then bounced him to the Oakland Oaks.[20] The Oaks didn't have room, either, so they sent him to Spokane. The Indians were surely glad to have him. Besides his hot start to the season, Risk had what Indians beat writer Bob Johnson called "one of the best dispositions of any guy in baseball."[21]

After the May 12 twin bill with Salem, Risk and his teammates took an overnight bus ride across Washington, over the Snoqualmie Pass, and into Seattle, where they caught a 7:00 a.m. boat for the six-and-a-half-hour ride to Victoria, a town on the southern tip of Vancouver Island in British

Columbia. The Indians were joined by a new pitcher north of the border. The San Diego Padres sent the Indians Joe Faria, a twenty-seven-year-old right-hander from Oakland, California. Faria's spring training ledger, which included a win over the Chicago Cubs, drew rave reviews from sportswriters. But so far during the regular season, he had thrown only two innings of mop-up relief for the Padres. Finally, manager Pepper Martin—of St. Louis Cardinals and Gashouse Gang fame—told a frustrated Faria he was going to start the first game of a doubleheader. The hurler excitedly arrived at the ballpark early, only to find out that Martin had changed his mind. Faria furiously changed out of his uniform and watched the game from the stands. Martin fined him $50 and, in turn, Faria asked to be traded or released.[22] The Padres obliged by sending him to Spokane. Faria already knew many players on the Indians' roster; he was childhood friends with Cadinha and had played with Cole, Lohrke, and Martinez at various points in his baseball journey.

The visitors from Spokane found the Victoria Athletics' pitching to their liking in the series opener, raking seventeen hits in a 10–2 blowout. Levi McCormack led the charge with four base hits; Picetti, Paterson, and Lohrke each chipped in with three.

The next day, Picetti sat in his room at the Hotel Douglas and wrote to his mother. He described Vancouver Island's "miserable weather" and reassured her that he was eating well.[23] In that night's game, Faria got his first starting pitching assignment for the Indians and held Victoria to one run through nine innings. Athletics starter Bob Jensen was just as sharp, however. Spokane trailed, 1–0, with two outs in the top of the ninth inning when Freddie Martinez blasted a clutch game-tying home run. In the twelfth inning, a Picetti RBI single plated one of four Spokane runs. The Indians held on to win, 5–3.

Spokane pulverized Victoria the next two nights, winning by scores of 8–1 and 23–1. Paterson, James, McCormack, and Picetti all clubbed round-trippers. The latter game got so out of hand that Victoria used a pair of position players on the mound and Cole replaced his starting outfield with pitchers Kinnaman, Powers, and Cadinha.

Victoria put up a more respectable fight on May 17 but still could muster only two runs off Kinnaman. Paterson, Martinez, and McCormack each homered for Spokane in the Indians' 5–2 win. The two teams then closed out the seven-game series with a Saturday doubleheader. Lohrke, hitting second in the batting order, launched a pair of home runs in the lid-lifter. The Athletics salvaged a game and broke a ten-game losing streak in the finale, edging the Indians 11–10.

The citizens of Victoria were not enthusiastic about the quality of baseball exhibited by the home team. Sam Collins was irate after learning that the average attendance for the series was 849.[24] The low turnout cut into profits of the Indians, who, as the visiting team, would receive only slightly more than the league minimum of $100 per game.

British Columbia laws prohibited baseball on Sundays, so the Indians enjoyed a day off before beginning a seven-game series across the Strait of Georgia in Vancouver on Monday, May 20. The Capilanos, named after Emil Sick's brewery of the same name, played in a ballpark at Fifth Avenue and Hemlock Street near Granville Island. In the opener, thirteen hits ceded by Dick Powers and three miscues by the Indians' defense doomed Spokane in a 7–1 defeat. Spokane turned the tables on Vancouver the next night, 9–2. Picetti, Lohrke, and Risk each reached base safely three times, and Paterson crushed a 410-foot home run over the right-center field wall for the victors.[25] Faria picked up his second win and the Indians (16–10) moved into a first-place tie with Salem.

The series continued to seesaw the following night. The Capilanos built an 8–1 lead through six frames against starter Gus Hallbourg. Doug Oliver entered in relief and added gas to the fire, surrendering another seven runs in a third of an inning. Mel Cole finally put himself on the mound to get the final five outs, absorbing four more runs in the process. As the *Vancouver Sun* put it, "the Capilanos threw everything but their bat boy at the tribe" in a 19–1 trouncing.[26]

Tempers flared the next night as the Indians looked to even up the series. Cole, typically mild-mannered off the field, became riled up in the top of the sixth inning when Indians catcher Bob Paulson, back in the lineup after missing time with a foot injury, hit a line drive down the line that sailed over the fence. The umpires ruled that the ball was foul. Cole was still simmering when Paulson's next batted ball—a would-be RBI base hit down the third-base line—was also called foul. Cole threw his hat in the air, jumped up and down, then charged umpire Jack Rice with his right fist cocked. Several Spokane players held Cole back, but he wriggled loose, cocked his fist, and made another lunge toward Rice. This process repeated numerous times before Cole calmed down and accepted his ejection. In a surprising turn of events, Rice then consulted the base umpire, who did not have a good look at the play in question. Nonetheless, the call was reversed, resulting in arguments from the Capilanos bench. The game finally resumed under protest by Vancouver.[27] The hotly debated base hit by Paulson came amid a three-run rally by the Indians, who held on to win, 4–2, behind another strong outing by Cadinha. Cole's tirade resulted in a $25 fine by league president Robert Abel.[28]

Holman "Pee Wee" Bass drew the starting pitching assignment for Spokane in the first game of a series-ending twin bill. The thirty-nine-year-old soft-tossing righty had first pitched professionally two decades earlier and had previously hurled baseballs for the House of David, an early twentieth-century barnstorming team founded by a religious community of the same name.[29] Bass, who earned his moniker because of his diminutive five-feet-six, 125-pound stature, had also worked as a scout for the Boston Red Sox.[30] He entered the game with a 1–2 record and seventeen walks in 29⅓ innings.[31] Bass's status on the team became even more tenuous after Vancouver torched him for seven tallies in 3⅔ innings in a 14–5 rout. Bob Kinnaman, who had split his first four decisions, tamed the Vancouver bats in the nightcap but suffered from a lack of run support and took the loss, 2–1. In the series finale, Vic Picetti raked three hits, including a home run, but the Capilanos came out ahead, 5–4. After dropping five of seven in the series, the Indians (17–14) returned home in fourth place.

The Indians' play through the first month of the season had been uneven. The pitching of Cadinha had been superb and the offensive production from the infielders and outfielders robust. George Risk led the club with a .378 average, and Freddie Martinez was only five points behind. McCormack, Lohrke, Paterson, and Picetti were all hitting above .300.[32] But there was a lack of depth on the pitching staff, little offensive production from the catching corps, and the infield turned the fewest double plays in the league.[33] As Collins looked for ways to improve his club, he got wind that the Sacramento Solons of the PCL had recently parted ways with Ben Geraghty, a thirty-one-year-old sure-handed infielder with big league experience. Collins inked Geraghty to a contract, possibly with intentions of having him take over as manager.

The Indians next began an eight-game home series against the lowly Victoria Athletics on May 28. Before the first game, the Indians cut backup infielder Bill Dunn and catcher Neil Clifford, who were hitting .147 and .204, respectively.[34] Both were summarily snatched up by the Athletics, who were in last place with an 8–25 record and desperate to upgrade a floundering roster. Dunn and Clifford reported to the visitors' dugout and both were inserted into Victoria's lineup to face Cadinha. Jack Lohrke (three for four with two runs scored) and Vic Picetti (two for four, including a triple) led the Indians' offensive charge in support of Cadinha, who improved to 5–0 with a dominant two-hit shutout. Ironically, Dunn and Clifford accounted for Victoria's only hits.

Cadinha's season ledger now included a one-hitter and a pair of two-hitters. The twenty-four-year-old hurler was flourishing for Spokane and was among the top pitchers in the Western International League (WIL). But this was not Cadinha's first go-around in the circuit. Before the war, the Oakland native signed with the Pacific Coast League's San Francisco Seals. The Seals wanted Cadinha to gain experience at a lower league, so they sent him to Tacoma, where he won twenty-six games during two seasons.

Had blooper reels existed in 1946, the Athletics' play the following night would have provided enough footage for a full-length feature. The comedy of errors began in the bottom of the first inning, when Bob Paterson hit a lazy fly ball down the right-field line. Victoria's right fielder, Pete Hughes, failed to make the catch and then kicked the ball into foul territory near a portable batting cage. He retrieved the ball and tried to throw it back toward the infield, but the ball ricocheted off the cage and was redirected over the fence, allowing Paterson to circle the bases.[35] Later in the game, Paterson stole home, much to the dismay of Clifford—the Athletics new catcher. As Clifford argued with the umpire, Freddie Martinez—the runner at second—took off for third. Clifford's throw to third sailed into left field, allowing Martinez to scamper home.

Though the first eight innings were entertaining to the Ferris Field faithful, the most bizarre play of the game came in the final frame with the Athletics at the plate, trailing by twelve. Victoria's Al Steele was on first base with one out and Lester Mulcahy at the plate. Mulcahy hit a blast into the right-center field gap. Right fielder Bob James ran it down, tossed it to Paterson, who threw to Risk, who relayed the ball to Lohrke at third. Lohrke stepped on third base and Steele, who appeared to have scored, was ruled out for missing the bag. Lohrke then threw across the diamond to Picetti, and Mulcahy was ruled out because he never touched first. The umpires ran for their dressing room as the Victoria players howled in protest.[36] It was quite possibly the only 9–8–6–5–3 double play in the history of professional baseball. All told, the Athletics committed eight errors in the game. Between the miscues and Spokane's seventeen hits, it was a wonder that the Indians plated *only* fourteen runs.

Vic Picetti longed for home. Though he was having success on the field, his time away from the park was monotonous, and the bus travel was brutal. A year before, he had experienced the relative luxury of the PCL, traveling by train to the West Coast's premiere cities. Plus, he had played near home, where he could see his family regularly. Now, he had been away for two months. Spokane was far from San Francisco, literally and figuratively, but he tried to make the best of the situation while supporting his mother and siblings back home. He found that his salary did not go far, particularly during homestands in Spokane, where he had to pay for his own housing. During the first month of the season, Picetti had stayed at the relatively pricey Halliday Hotel when the team was in Spokane. Now that the Indians had a two-week homestand, he and two teammates found a cabin that was more budget friendly. He wrote his mother on May 30:

> Dear Ma,
>
> Well, here we are at Sorenson's cabins, about a mile outside of town. We have a very nice place, and we are doing our own cooking. Doug Oliver, Dick Powers are the two other fellows with me. I have a picture I am getting developed and will send to you as soon as I get it. We get paid Saturday, and will send you some money. . . .
>
> Our money goes pretty fast up here between room and board and everything. We are home for 2 weeks now. We won the first two games of our series so far. I have 5 for 9 already. I am batting .321. I hit another home run in Vancouver Saturday night. Coming home on the bus after the game Saturday I got sick all the way to Spokane. I had a stomach ache. I had lumbago in my back and have been going to the doctors every day. It's getting better now. . . .
>
> Haven't been doing much of anything. Seen quite a few shows, saw *The Blue Dahlia* the other day. Also saw *Gilda*. Sure is a lousy league up here.

Beans Marionetti and Vic Buccola are with Victoria now. Everybody would rather go home.

Well, I guess we'll go to bed now, so I'll see you soon, and take care of yourself.

Love,

Jun

P.S. Old San Francisco is the best place.[37]

Picetti was clearly not enamored with Class B baseball, particularly given that the Indians had mostly played the circuit's two weakest teams—Victoria and Vancouver. Later in the homestand, reliever Doug Oliver broke his thumb and returned home to California. Without a third person to share rent at the cabin, Picetti and Powers moved back to the Halliday Hotel.

Picetti and his teammates banged out twenty-three hits in a Memorial Day doubleheader sweep of Victoria. Martinez's three-run homer in the nightcap was the Indians' first home run of the season at spacious Ferris Field.[38] Like George Risk, Martinez came to Spokane with confidence after playing alongside major leaguers during his military service. Frederick Thomas Martinez, twenty-five, hailed from San Diego, California. His mother, the former Frances Rodriguez, was born in Mexico and moved to California at age six. She married Thomas Martinez, a California-born member of the San Pasqual Band of Mission Indians, in 1919.[39] Frederick was their second of ten children. By his teenage years, he had grown into a standout ballplayer for a San Diego American Legion team and earned a professional contract. In the summer of 1940, Frederick, often called "Freddie" or "Marty," played professionally for Brooklyn Dodgers affiliates in Landis, North Carolina, and Americus, Georgia. During his nearly three years in the navy, Martinez played for the Naval Air Station Kaneohe Bay Klippers, a service team that included New York Giants first baseman Johnny Mize, Chicago Cubs catcher Marv Felderman, and Brooklyn Dodgers righty Hugh Casey.[40] The Klippers competed against teams with future Hall of Famers Stan Musial, Pee Wee Reese, and Joe DiMaggio. After his discharge from the service, Martinez joined the Bellingham Bells of the semipro Van-Bell League in 1945. The solidly built five-feet-nine, 180-pound right-hander possessed the ability to play infield or outfield. With second baseman Ben Geraghty on his way to Spokane, Martinez's versatility would soon come in handy.

Collins' roster maneuvering continued on the last day of May with the release of Pee Wee Bass and signing of catcher Irv Konopka. That night, the Indians were in danger of suffering their first loss of the series, trailing Victoria, 3–2, to start the bottom of the ninth. Geraghty made his Spokane debut as a pinch hitter and reached safely to start a rally. Later in the inning, Paterson, who had struck out in each of his first four at-bats, stepped to the plate with the bases loaded. The lanky center fielder delivered a line drive to the left-center field gap that scored the tying and winning runs.

As the calendar turned to June, Spokane was tied with Wenatchee for second place and trailed first-place Salem by only one game. With a lot of baseball left to play, the WIL was still very much up for grabs. The Indians, now with Geraghty on board and another former Brooklyn Dodger soon to come, were prime contenders to win the pennant.

7

HARTJE JOINS RACE FOR PENNANT

The Spokane Indians lost to Victoria on Saturday, June 1, then resumed their dominance over the cellar dwellers in a series-concluding doubleheader the following day. In the first game, Bob James recorded five hits—one of which was a grand slam—and drove in seven of the Indians' sixteen runs. Milt Cadinha remained undefeated following a ten-strikeout complete game performance in Spokane's 5–2 victory in the nightcap. Jack Lohrke stroked five hits on the day, including a home run. On defense, the third sacker showed no fear when he toppled over the rail attempting to catch a foul ball in the first game. Lohrke "hustles like an office boy who expects to become a railroad president," wrote the *Spokesman-Review*.[1]

Lohrke and James each finished the series fifteen for thirty-two, an average of .469. After feasting on Victoria's pitching for two of the last three weeks, the Indians' lineup, excluding the pitchers, was hitting a robust .330.[2]

Two days later, the Indians welcomed the Tacoma Tigers to town. The visitors took a seemingly secure 10–4 lead into the bottom of the ninth inning in the series opener. Many of the 2,667 who paid to see the game had already conceded defeat and left Ferris Field. The men in the home dugout had not given up, however. The Indians proceeded to bat around, scoring seven runs on five hits, a walk, and two errors. Mel Cole delivered the game-tying single and Lohrke drove home the winning run to seal a dramatic come-from-behind victory.[3]

The next night's tilt was played in a constant drizzle that failed to faze starting pitcher Bob Kinnaman, who struck out nine and went the distance in Spokane's 8–4 triumph. Levi McCormack ignited the offensive attack with a three-run double. The light rain turned into a deluge just as the last out was recorded. Meanwhile, Victoria's surprising doubleheader sweep of Salem moved Spokane into first place.[4]

The Indians and Tigers were idle on June 6. Spokane native Bing Crosby was in town with Bob Hope for a fundraiser at Downriver Golf Course. The pair of entertainers had played more than one hundred rounds of golf around the country to sell war bonds and raise money for various charities.[5] Vic Picetti used the day off to catch the new crime film noir *The Dark Corner*, starring Lucille Ball, William Bendix, and Mark Stevens. The picture was shown at the State Theatre, an eight-hundred-seat venue on Sprague Street, which would later be refurbished and renamed after Crosby.

When the series resumed the next night, Ben Geraghty made his first start for the Indians and went three for four with a double and triple. Picetti also recorded three hits and Lohrke hit safely in all four of his at-bats. Dick Powers was credited with the win in Spokane's 12–5 victory.[6] Tacoma captured two of the final three games of the series, dropping the Indians to third place in the tightly packed Western International League.

Two days later, the Indians and Tigers met up again on Tacoma's home turf. While the Indians were on the road, Ferris Field hosted the Portland Rosebuds and Seattle Steelheads of the newly formed West Coast Negro Baseball Association. A crowd of fifteen hundred watched Seattle rout Portland, 11–2. The league, which was organized by track star Jesse Owens and Harlem Globetrotters founder Abe Saperstein, would disband a month later.

In Tacoma, the Tigers beat the Indians in the first two games before soggy weather forced postponement of the next three. Vic Picetti used the downtime to catch *Diary of a Chambermaid* with Paulette Goddard and Burgess Meredith, a film about a gold-digging maid who hopes to marry a rich husband. When Picetti scribbled a letter to his mother on June 12, his review of the film was brief: "kind of lousy." He used the same adjective to describe to league's umpires and also lamented how quickly his

$600-per-month salary could disappear: "By the time you pay for hotels and meals and such, it sure goes."[7]

The rain had stopped, but the grass was still slick when the series resumed with a doubleheader. Three would-be routine fly balls fell in because Spokane outfielders slipped on the turf.[8] The Indians' frustration with the league's subpar umpiring boiled over. Cole, Martinez, and Picetti were all tossed from one of the games for arguing.[9] Cole's third ejection of the season earned him a $10 fine and three-game suspension.[10] "There's little doubt that the eight men assigned to call the balls and strikes and the outs this year are far below pre-war standards," opined Bob Johnson of the *Spokane Chronicle*.[11]

The Indians limped back to Spokane in fifth place, now six and a half games behind the red-hot Salem Senators, who had won ten of eleven. The Indians' catching situation remained fluid as the team prepared to begin an important seven-game series against Salem. The Indians had recently debuted new backstop Irv Konopka, who was serving in a reserve role. Konopka, the son of Polish immigrants and a native of Milwaukee, Wisconsin, was fresh out of the University of Idaho, where he was a member of the Vandals' wrestling team, played catcher for the baseball squad, and battled in the trenches as an offensive lineman on the gridiron. Built like a phone booth, the hefty six-feet-two tackle had impressed enough on the football field to be drafted by the Detroit Lions in 1943.[12] After serving in the army during the war, the twenty-six-year-old returned to Idaho to complete his degree and resume his athletic endeavors. He planned to play football for Detroit in the fall. Even with Konopka added as catching depth, Sam Collins sought more offense at the position. To that end, he replaced light-hitting Bob Paulson with Chris Hartje, who, seven years earlier, had caught for the Brooklyn Dodgers.

Christian Henry Hartje was born and raised in San Francisco. His parents, Dietrich and Marie, immigrated to America from Germany before the turn of the twentieth century. Dietrich worked as a laborer at American Can Company while Marie stayed home and raised the couple's eleven children. By the time Chris was a teenager, the brown-haired, blue-eyed youngster had developed into an excellent catcher.

When he was eighteen, Hartje signed with the New York Yankees and rose through the ranks of the minor leagues over the next several seasons.

He put himself on the map as a legitimate major league prospect in 1936, hitting .323 for the Oakland Oaks. He followed that standout campaign by hitting .292 for the Kansas City Blues, the Yankees' top farm team. Hartje returned to Kansas City for a second season in 1938 but endured several physical maladies that kept him out of action for stretches of time. He missed two weeks after taking a foul tip to the finger in a spring training game, suffered a nasty bout of salami sandwich–induced food poisoning, and then sustained another injury to his throwing hand.[13] All told, he was limited to only forty-four games with the Blues. Nonetheless, he played well enough when able to be named to the circuit's All-Star team, which was scheduled to play on July 14 in Indianapolis. He would have been in the same All-Star lineup as Ted Williams of the Minneapolis Millers, but Hartje left the Blues on July 7 and subsequently missed the exhibition because of the alleged death of his mother.[14] Given that Marie Hartje did not die until 1952, the reports were erroneous or Hartje, who was "known to become afflicted with homesickness," made up the excuse to visit family.[15] In either case, he never returned to Kansas City that season. In August, the Royals loaned Hartje to the PCL's Hollywood Stars, with whom he appeared in ten games.

Chris married Grace "Holly" Wolff in January 1939. The pair of San Franciscans had first met at a wedding. Both were in other relationships at the time, but they hit it off and soon became an item. The newlyweds did not have two nickels to rub together, but Chris still had dreams of making a living in baseball. The young couple lived with Holly's parents, Louis and Lillian, in a small house that Louis originally built near San Francisco's Ocean Beach. After the 1906 earthquake, Louis used a team of horses to move the house to Fifth Avenue near Geary, just a few blocks north of Golden Gate Park.

Bill Dickey, a future Hall of Famer, was entrenched at catcher for the Yankees, so Hartje became an expendable commodity. In February 1939, the Bronx Bombers cashed in on their young prospect, selling Hartje and two other minor leaguers to the Brooklyn Dodgers for $50,000.[16] The Dodgers were managed by Leo Durocher, who earned the nickname "the Lip" as a player because of his incessant yammering and never-ending verbal assaults directed at his opponents. Durocher's grit, determination, and win-at-all-cost mentality kept him employed in the game for nearly a half-century. His personality was the polar opposite of Hartje, a Californian who exuded a mild-mannered, happy-go-lucky vibe. To Durocher, this came across as lazy. The skipper told Hartje that it was fine by him if he wanted to stay in the minors and work for peanut money.[17] When it came time for roster cuts, the young backstop was jettisoned to the Montreal Royals, a Dodgers minor league affiliate.

Hartje performed well for the Royals, hitting .296 with three home runs in 116 games. A reporter from the *Montreal Gazette* observed that "Chris laughs all the time, for life to him is one long joke. He takes practically nothing seriously."[18] Though he may have exhibited a carefree attitude off the field, he demonstrated toughness between the white lines. When the team's backup catcher was injured during the dog days of August, Hartje caught all thirty-seven innings of back-to-back doubleheaders.[19]

Hartje received his big break when Dodgers starting catcher Babe Phelps suffered a broken thumb in early September of 1939. To take Phelps's place, Brooklyn summoned Hartje, who made his major league debut in a pressure-packed situation versus the New York Giants at Ebbets Field on September 9. The Dodgers trailed, 3–2, and had runners on first and third with no outs in the bottom of the eighth inning. Durocher sent the rookie up to pinch hit for Art Parks against former twenty-game winner Cliff Melton, who was pitching in relief that day. Hartje pulled the second pitch he saw down the left-field line for a double, scoring the tying and go-ahead runs. Brooklyn went on to win, 8–3.

Five days after his heroic game-winning pinch hit, Hartje received his first starting assignment at Pittsburgh's Forbes Field, joining fellow Bay Area natives Dolph Camilli and Cookie Lavagetto in Durocher's lineup. Hartje recorded three hits in four at-bats and was lauded for his defense. Durocher noticed more pep in Hartje's step and improvements in the batter's box compared to spring training. "I guess he must have got mad when I sent him to Montreal," said the skipper.[20] A taste of success in the majors provided Hartje with enough confidence to declare, "I'm going to make this club as a regular next year."[21] He appeared in a total of nine games for the Dodgers and accrued five hits in sixteen at-bats for a .313 batting average.

Hartje went to Florida the following spring looking to make good on his prediction of being the Dodgers' top catcher. A pair of home runs against the Reds on March 9 appeared to help his cause, but a raging case of tonsillitis later in the spring derailed his tryout. He improved with treatment and avoided surgery but shortly thereafter was optioned back to Montreal.

Even if he had stayed healthy, Hartje was unlikely to have stuck with the Dodgers. General manager Larry MacPhail, like Durocher, liked Hartje as a player but was not fond of his carefree attitude and propensity to break curfew.[22] Hartje did not mind being seen around town with a pint of beer, and word of his late-night carousing made its way to his bosses.[23] After a stint as Montreal's backup catcher, the Dodgers sold him to the Syracuse Chiefs in early June. He yearned to play for a West Coast team so he could be closer to home but had no choice but to suit up for the team that held his contract.[24]

Hartje remained with Syracuse through the 1942 season and demonstrated more hustle and determination than in previous years. Perhaps it was maturity or the realization that his chance of making it back to the major leagues was slipping away. "Maybe he's started to think about himself the last little while and has become serious about baseball for the first time in his life," remarked a former teammate. "He's sure a lot different than he used to be. If he keeps it up, he might get another chance up in the big leagues yet."[25] During the 1941 season, Hartje played a game with appendicitis. He fought through the pain, at one point calling time so he could vomit before returning to his position behind home plate. After the game, he went to the hospital and required an emergency appendectomy.[26]

Hartje enlisted in the coast guard in March 1943. He was stationed in the East Bay and played ball for a coast guard team called the Sea Lions while serving for the next three years. He was discharged with a rank of seaman first class. Hartje likely hooked up with Spokane through his connections to Dutch Anderson and Bob Paterson, both of whom he knew in San Francisco. At thirty-one, Hartje was not quite ready to give up on his baseball career.

After years of studying the game and learning under Casey Stengel, Ben Geraghty got his first taste of managing, filling in for the suspended Mel Cole during the first three games of Spokane's series versus Salem. The Indians got off to an auspicious start, outlasting the Senators, 10–9, in the opener on June 18.

The Indians performed one of baseball's rarest feats the following night. The Senators had runners on first and second with no outs in the first inning. Vern Reynolds hit a line drive to shortstop George Risk, who threw to Geraghty covering second. Geraghty whipped the ball to Picetti at first base to complete a triple play. Starting pitcher Dick Powers faltered on the mound, however, and Spokane's defensive trifecta was overshadowed by Salem's decisive 7–1 victory. George Lyden's 4⅓ innings of one-run ball in relief would earn him a long-awaited starting assignment later in the series.[27]

Hartje made his Spokane debut in the third game of the series and contributed two walks and a two-run single to propel the Indians to victory. Milt Cadinha, whose home ERA on the season was a superb 1.30, improved to 7–0 at Ferris Field.[28] The next day, Salem evened the series at two games per side with a 9–3 win.

Picetti, hitless in his last three games, seemed to be pressing.[29] The brief slump could have been a blip that all players experience or perhaps related to a bit of homesickness. Vic undoubtedly missed his family and was counting the days until late July when his fiancée, mother, and younger brother were scheduled to drive up for a visit. Vic and Betty planned to solidify plans for a September wedding.

Vic wrote his mother on Friday, June 21:

> Dear Ma,
>
> Well only one more month, and you'll be in Spokane. Sure is warm up here and will really be warm when you get here. Haven't been doing very good, but just have to keep trying I suppose. . . .
>
> I'll get you a cabin. I think I can get one with two bedrooms, kitchen, bathroom, and sofa and such out by the ballpark. We had one there for a while and it wasn't bad. Cost $24 a week. . . .
>
> Saw *Hoodlum Saint* with William Powell and Esther Williams, and also a dual horror show, which wasn't bad . . . outside of that haven't been doing anything. . . . Well, I'll see you soon, so take care of yourself, and say hello to everybody.
>
> Love always,
> Junior[30]

"Vic was the ultimate first baseman, but he was terribly homesick," recalled Milt Cadinha years later. "And when he went into a slump, he just got down on himself. He was such a quiet kid, nice as can be. Everybody thought he was wonderful. But he was lonely up in Spokane."[31] Sam Collins and Dwight Aden, sympathetic to the teenager's plight, came up with a plan. When the team got to Bremerton for their next series, they would send Picetti home to San Francisco for a week to see his family.

Picetti got a much-needed breather the next night. Freddie Martinez, who had been seeing action in right field in place of Bob James, filled in at first base. The first four batters in the Indians' lineup—Geraghty, Risk, Paterson, and McCormack—combined for eight hits and provided adequate run support for starter Gus Hallbourg in Spokane's 7–5 victory.

The series had gone back-and-forth through five games with the Indians holding a 3–2 advantage heading into a series-concluding twin bill on Sunday, June 23. Because of a threat of rain, only 574 fans showed up for the afternoon game. Hartje gave the Indians an early lead with a two-run double in the first inning. Lyden toed the rubber for Spokane and was let down by his defense, which committed four errors in the first three innings, allowing Salem to pull ahead, 6–2. The Indians, trailing 9–4 entering the bottom of the ninth, attempted a late rally. Irv Konopka, who had entered at catcher after Hartje suffered a bruised knee, hit a home run that was still rising as it sailed over the left-field fence. The blast was Konopka's first professional base hit. Consecutive hits by Geraghty, Risk, and Paterson plated two more runs, cutting the deficit to 9–7. Spokane would not get any closer.

In between games, the Indians gathered on the field for a team photo, which was snapped by Lawrence Numbers of Nu-Art Studio. The Indians' publicity man, Ken Hunter, usually arranged for the team photo near the end of the season, but for some reason he decided to do it earlier this year.

With the series even at three games per side, the nightcap would decide the series. With Milt Cadinha on the bump, the odds were certainly in the Indians' favor. Konopka made his first start at catcher, and Picetti returned to the lineup at first base. Spokane jumped out to a four-run lead through five innings, in part because of Jack Lohrke's 380-foot home run that nearly destroyed a clock above the left-center field wall.[32] It was the third basemen's fourth long ball of the season. Wildness plagued Cadinha in the sixth, allowing Salem to tie the game. The Indians regained a two-run lead with tallies in the sixth and seventh, but Salem put up a five-spot off Cadinha in the eighth to pull back ahead, 9–7.

In the bottom of the ninth, Konopka reached on an error to start the inning. After pinch hitter Martinez popped out, Geraghty and Risk followed with consecutive singles, scoring Konopka. Paterson then rapped a double to the left-center field gap, scoring Geraghty with the tying run. The Senators intentionally walked Levi McCormack to set up a potential double play.

That brought up Bob James, who stroked a base hit to right field to win the game, 10–9. James was mobbed by his teammates in celebration. It was a true team win for Spokane, in which everyone in the starting lineup contributed. Geraghty recorded a pair of hits, Picetti singled and stole two bases, and Lohrke went four for five to raise his average to .345.

As fans filed out of Ferris Field after the rousing comeback, public address announcer Moose McGregor closed with these words: "and all the ballplayers wish you a good, good night and pleasant dreams."[33]

Jack Lohrke was hitting the daylights out of the ball, had walked thirteen times more than he struck out, and was playing sterling defense at the hot corner. "One of these seasons in the not too distant future we're going to be asking that guy for autographs," remarked Bob Kinnaman.[34] Two days earlier, Collins spoke with executives of the San Diego Padres and put in a good word for his third baseman.[35]

Lohrke was far from the only Spokane player thriving, however. Newcomer Geraghty had reverted to his youthful form, hitting .328 while stabilizing the infield defense. Martinez was leading the team with a .353 average, and Risk wasn't far behind at .349. McCormack and Paterson both boasted averages over .300. Picetti maintained a .285 average despite his recent slump and led the team with eight triples.

But there was something else about this Indians team—something beyond batting averages, wins, and losses. In the two months they had spent together, the club had formed close bonds. When Martinez had to leave a game because of an injury during the Salem series, the entire team went out and walked him off the field. And though they all had big-league aspirations, players would often encourage reporters to put out a good word about a teammate. "We can't recall that a player came to us in the dressing room once asking for a personal plug," wrote Bob Johnson. "It wasn't 'how many hits did I get,' but rather 'how did we do tonight?' If you don't think that's unusual, then you don't know ballplayers."[36]

Perhaps their altruism and affinity for one another resulted from their war experiences. And the mundane afternoons before games and long bus rides surely forged their friendships. "You always had a good time on the bus," recalled Gus Hallbourg year later. "You were always talking. We were a close-knit team."[37]

CHAPTER 7

After the raucous come-from-behind win against the league-leading Senators the previous night, the Indians' spirits were never higher as they prepared to travel west to face the Bremerton Bluejackets.

8

JUNE 24, 1946

Glen Berg looked at the board in the Washington Motor Coach Company garage and saw that the Spokane Indians' charter to Bremerton needed a driver. He had played a little amateur baseball himself and thought highly of the Indians prospects, so he decided to take the job. He had never driven the ball club before.

The calendar indicated it was summer, but it was unseasonably cool in Spokane. After temperatures had soared to nearly 90 a few days earlier, the thermometer on Monday, June 24, did not top 60. At 10:00 a.m., Berg, twenty-four, pulled bus number 306 into the Ferris Field parking lot, where he was met by Dwight Aden. The two loaded the bus with uniforms and equipment. The ballplayers were still buzzing about the previous night's triumph as they trickled in during the next ninety minutes. By 11:30 a.m., sixteen members of the team had boarded the twenty-five-passenger bus. Joe Faria, who owned a Buick convertible, had decided to drive separately with his wife; they invited another couple—Milt and Yuvonna Cadinha. It was the first time all season that Cadinha did not take the bus. Trainer Dutch Anderson, who usually accompanied the team, had traveled back to San Francisco. He was required to put in a full day's work at his other job as a pressman in order to keep his union benefits. Batboy Kenny Benshoof, who typically did not travel with the team on the road, had hoped to make the trip. He received permission from his parents but could not find Aden to get his final approval during the previous night's game.

Gus Hallbourg, Ben Geraghty, Mel Cole, and Bob James occupied the first two rows. Jack Lohrke picked the window seat on the left side of the bus and was joined by Levi McCormack. Fred Martinez and Bob Kinnaman sat across on the right side of the bus. Vic Picetti and Bob Paterson occupied the seat behind Lohrke and McCormack. George Risk, Chris Hartje, George Lyden, Dick Powers, Irv Konopka, and Pete Barisoff took seats in the back half of the bus. Barisoff had dibs on a long bench-style seat in the back where he could stretch out and take a nap. After all, it was a trip of more than three hundred miles that would take the better part of the day.

The bus sputtered southwest out of Spokane on US Route 10, also known as the Sunset Highway, a two-lane road that connected Spokane to Seattle. Interstate 90, which would make travel across the state a quicker and less perilous trek, was still decades away from completion. During the next several hours, Berg steered the coach through varied terrain. Just outside of Spokane, the road cut through a ponderosa pine forest. Closer to Sprague, the tree line gave way to rolling green and gold hills. Past Ritzville, where the team stopped for a quick rest break, the road pointed due west, past endless wheat fields dotted by the occasional farmhouse. After Moses Lake, Route 10 descended into a visually stunning canyon, where brown basalt cliffs rose from the Columbia River.

While the ball team slowly made their way across Washington, back in Spokane, Sam Collins received a telegram from San Diego. The Padres, who held the rights to Lohrke, wanted their red-hot prospect to report to San Diego posthaste. Collins's first thought was to send a wire to Bremerton but then remembered that the team was planning to stop in Ellensburg for dinner.[1] He gave the task of notifying Lohrke to Aden, who phoned the state police and asked them to contact the Ellensburg police department.

By late afternoon, the bus had reached Ellensburg, just past the halfway point to Bremerton. While the team ate dinner at Webster's Café, Berg took the bus to the Washington Motor Coach Company's local garage, where he complained that the engine was running poorly, resulting in a faulty vacuum brake booster. Mechanics changed the gas line, but in Berg's assessment, it "didn't seem to do any good."[2] As the players ate, a police officer found the team and told Lohrke to call the Indians' front office. "You've been recalled by San Diego," said the voice on the other end. "Come back to Spokane as soon as you can."[3]

As the team reboarded the bus after dinner, Lohrke grabbed his belongings, shook hands, and said good-byes. "I wanted to wish them all well, particularly my roommates Freddie Martinez and Bob James," Lohrke remembered. "Being called up was a big deal for me. In the Coast League I'd be riding trains."[4]

Lyden asked Geraghty to switch seats, taking the first seat on the right. Geraghty grabbed a seat farther back, a decision that would have life-changing ramifications. The bus rolled out of Ellensburg around 6:00 p.m., heading west and gradually approaching the Cascades, a mountain range stretching more than seven hundred miles from British Columbia to northern California. As the bus passed through the towns of Cle Elum and Easton, jagged snow-covered peaks and pine-covered slopes loomed ahead. Some players dozed off while others chatted.

Traversing the Cascades required a drive over Snoqualmie Pass, which had long been the region's preferred east-west route. At slightly more than three thousand feet, it had a lower elevation and lighter grades that made for a less treacherous passage than other areas in the North Cascades. Native Americans were the first to establish a trail there centuries earlier. In the mid-nineteenth century, the discovery of gold in British Columbia's Fraser Canyon attracted droves of miners, who crossed the pass by foot or on horseback. As more emigrants traveled west in subsequent decades, a wagon road was gradually constructed. Automobiles first crossed Snoqualmie Pass in 1905, but conditions were so poor that the trip took multiple days. A compacted gravel road, part of the Sunset Highway, was completed in 1915. The journey was still by no means easy, however. Shortly after the new road opened, a drive from downtown Seattle to Yakima—a distance of 170 miles—took ten hours.[5] By 1926, the Washington State Highway Department had straightened curves and reduced steep grades west of the summit and the two-lane road was designated as US Route 10.

At around 7:30 p.m., the Indians' bus reached the pass and began to descend the western slope as rain fell from the dusk sky. Just past the summit, the bus chugged downhill on a straight stretch of road. Berg later estimated that he was traveling at twenty-eight miles per hour. One witness, however, reported that the bus passed him around that same time, traveling at more than forty-five or fifty miles an hour.[6] Gus Hallbourg looked out the window and saw a deep ravine to the right. He remarked to Bob Kinnaman,

"This would be a hell of a place to go over, wouldn't it?"[7] Berg exchanged headlight blinks with an oncoming Inland Motor Freight truck, each signaling that the road ahead was clear. Moments later, Berg saw a black sedan approaching on the wrong side of the road, its headlights shining directly in front of him through the mist. Levi McCormack and Ben Geraghty saw the same glare of headlights. Berg later said he believed the car was passing a truck.[8]

Berg maneuvered the bus onto the narrow shoulder of the road, simultaneously trying to avoid the oncoming vehicle and the cable guardrail. He made a split-second decision to step on the gas rather than the brakes for fear of skidding on the wet pavement. As the wrong-sided driver and bus converged, the sedan clipped the front end of the bus. Barisoff, sleeping in the back of the bus, was awoken by the impact. Berg managed to get the front wheels back on the road, but the rear tires remained on the soft shoulder. He struggled as the front end veered back onto the shoulder. The bus collided with the protective guard cables, then began to take out concrete guard posts like bowling pins.

There was an eerie stillness as the bus suddenly broke through the cables and went over the edge.[9] McCormack and Geraghty dove to the floor, grabbed seat brackets, and held on for their lives. Hallbourg crouched and grabbed the seat next to him that had been vacated by Lohrke. The bottom seemingly fell out of the bus as it left the road. "It was like jumping out of a 10 story building," described Barisoff. Geraghty thought to himself, "This is it. We haven't a chance."[10] Most areas of the Cascades along Highway 10 were densely covered with Douglas fir, western hemlock, and red alder, but the bus happened to go off a stretch of road where there were no trees to halt its descent. As it hurtled into the abyss, the bus hit a boulder and flipped over. Windows shattered and sparks began to fly. The gas tank along one side broke open. The bus struck another boulder as it rolled downhill and burst into flames. The sound of twisting metal broke the serenity of the evergreen forest and white noise of the nearby Snoqualmie River. "I've never heard such hell," said McCormack.[11]

As the bus tumbled, some players managed to hang on to their seats while others were helplessly tossed about. Ben Geraghty felt like he was in an egg beater before being hurled with such force that he was propelled out of a window.[12] Dick Powers and Vic Picetti were among the others who were ejected. One player was thrown 120 feet through a dense thicket beyond where the bus came to rest. Geraghty still had a window frame around his neck when he regained consciousness on the side of the mountain. He saw something on fire twenty feet away and realized it was one of his teammates. As he got closer, he recognized that it was Chris Hartje. Geraghty took off his jacket and smothered the flames. Geraghty then realized that his own scalp was hanging over his face, the result of a large *V*-shaped gash. He took off his undershirt and wrapped it around his head to control the bleeding, then looked down the mountain and saw the burning bus below.

A door, front axle and wheels, luggage, baseball equipment, and bodies were scattered on the rocky slope. The bus came to rest upright, straddling a log three hundred feet below the road. The battered vehicle, its front end embroiled in flames, looked like a crumpled aluminum can. Only a boulder and small area of flat ground kept it from plunging another 180 feet into the South Fork of the Snoqualmie River.[13] When the bus stopped rolling, Berg remained in the driver's seat, gripping the steering wheel, his clothes on fire. He stumbled out of the wreckage while simultaneously trying to extinguish the flames on his arms. Hallbourg, who had been knocked unconscious, came to his senses in time to squeeze through a window that was narrower than his hips. His leather jacket helped protect his arms from the jagged glass of a shattered window. McCormack escaped in a similar manner. The two shook hands, happy to see one another still alive.[14] Their momentary relief was halted by cries from above, where Vic Picetti was lying on a boulder.

Barisoff also blacked out during the crash and awoke to shouts from Irv Konopka. "Get me! I'm in the back of the bus! My back's busted! Get me!" he screamed.[15] Barisoff, dazed from a head injury, worked his way back to Konopka. Somehow, Barisoff managed to drag his hulking teammate out of the bus and away from the flames.

Geraghty, in a semiconscious state, felt helpless as he looked down at the burning pyre. "I knew I had no strength to do any good down there," he said, looking back. "All I could do was roll down in the flames."[16] Instead, he managed to crawl back up the hill to the road and waved down a motorist, who took him to a forestry service aid station.

Truck driver Nelson Allen witnessed the accident and was the first bystander on the scene. "I glanced in the rearview mirror after meeting the bus and saw the tail end of the bus going over the cliff," he told reporters.[17]

Allen tied a rope to a guardrail and lowered himself down the steep ravine. Two other men, including Glenn Spencer, followed. Allen found two victims lying directly beside the burning bus and dragged them farther away. He could hear screams coming from inside, but the inferno prohibited him from getting close enough to help. One player, engulfed in flames, stumbled out on his own. Allen quickly beat out the fire. When Spencer reached the scene, he helped Allen stamp out burning clothing of several victims. He found one man with an injured back. "Don't touch my back, don't move me!" the man shouted.[18] Another was sitting on a rock, sobbing and pleading for someone to help his friends.

Rescue vehicles, patrolmen, and volunteers swarmed to the scene, but reaching the victims proved to be an enormous challenge. Dozens of curious travelers on Highway 10 stopped to gawk, forcing rescue workers to navigate through a maze of obstacles. Darkening skies and steep terrain, slick and muddy from rainfall, further hampered rescue efforts. From the road, furious flames from the burning bus cast an eerie light on the horrific site below. Rescuers used flashlights and flares to light the way as they slid and stumbled down the embankment. Two officers were hurt by falling rocks as they helped recover a body and another had to be freed after becoming trapped under a heavy boulder. Policemen and forest service workers feebly attempted to fight the fire with shovelfuls of dirt. Others searched thickets of brush for other victims. Eventually, portable floodlights arrived from Olympia. The fiery bus continued to burn until past midnight, leaving the charred remains of the frame. Wearied rescuers used trolley cable to haul up victims, a process that continued until near dawn. Mel Cole, Bob James, Bob Kinnaman, Freddie Martinez, Bob Paterson, and George Risk were pronounced dead at the scene. Initial radio broadcasts reported Geraghty as one of the deceased.

Photographer John Bullard was driving on Aurora Avenue in Seattle when he heard news of the crash. He rushed to the scene and slid down the ravine using his coat as a glove to prevent friction burns to his hand from the rope while his other hand clung to his camera. One of Bullard's photos, a shot of the wreckage, appeared in the next day's *Seattle Post-Intelligencer*. The paper gave him $25 for his efforts.[19]

Ambulances and hearses transported the victims to Harborview Medical Center in Seattle, where doctors triaged the incoming mass casualty. "Tag this one for surgery," said one physician to an orderly after assessing George Lyden.[20] Nurses collected names and phone numbers of family from those who were coherent. Barisoff, whose injuries were the least severe of the survivors, helped to identify his teammates. He came to Vic Picetti, who sustained skull, femur, and pelvic fractures. He was pronounced dead in the ambulance on the way to the hospital. Tears streamed down Barisoff's face as he said, "It's Vic, the best player on the club."[21]

Jerry O'Brien sat in a Spokane newsroom on a quiet Monday night when a wire came across from the Associated Press bureau in Seattle. "Spokane: State patrol says chartered bus has gone off road at Snoqualmie Pass and that it may be Spokane baseball team. Please check club there soonest. Seattle."[22]

O'Brien quickly called *Spokesman-Review* sports editor Denny Spellecy, one floor below in the Review Building, then phoned Sam Collins: "Any chance it could be the team, Sam?" It was 8:30 p.m.—nine hours since the team left Spokane. Collins did the math in his head. "It couldn't be us then," he said. "We'd be over the pass by now."[23]

Collins made some phone calls and got wind that it could indeed be his boys. He called Aden. "I'm afraid it's us," he said.[24] Collins and Indians publicity man Ken Hunter went to the Associated Press newsroom in Spokane to see if there were any updates. Collins, Hunter, Spellecy, broadcaster Loyd Salt, and reporters Pat Patterson, Bob Johnson, and Bill Johnston stood in stunned silence as a bulletin came across the wire confirming that it was the Indians' bus and that several players were dead. Collins's first call was to his daughter, Joyce. "Get all the women up to the house," he said. "Don't let them do any calling . . . we'll call from there."[25]

At 11:00 p.m., Collins began the agonizing task of notifying wives and parents. A few hours later, Hunter and business manager Dwight Aden set out to find Mary Geraghty, who had just arrived in Spokane days earlier, along with her and Ben's three children. Mary did not have a radio and so did not hear the erroneous reports of her husband's death. Hunter and Aden had no luck stirring the hotel manager but found a car with New Jersey license plates and figured they must have the right room. Mary answered and received the news: Ben was injured but alive.

Faria and Cadinha had already crossed the Puget Sound on a ferry from Seattle to Bremerton when they heard news of the crash on the radio.

Shocked by the news, they hurried back to Seattle and went directly to the Harborview Medical Center to see the survivors.

Lohrke found out about the crash when he arrived in Spokane. "When I got back, I called the baseball office and told them, 'I'm back,'" he later remembered. "They said, 'forget about that. There's been a big bus crash and we think it's our boys.'"[26] He immediately sent a telegram to his parents: "Safe and sound. Back in Spokane. Love, Jack."[27] John and Marguerite Lohrke did not understand the context of their son's message until they read about the crash in the next day's paper. Both of Lohrke's roommates—Freddie Martinez and Bob James—were among the fatalities. In some ways, Lohrke's military service had conditioned him to navigate tragedy. "At that age, having been in combat, what's going to shock you?" he said years later.[28]

After a sleepless night, Aden and Hunter flew with Betty Lyden to Seattle at 6:00 a.m. the next morning. George Lyden had been unconscious since the accident and suffered from severe burns on his upper body. He succumbed to his injuries at 12:40 p.m.

Four of the surviving players were admitted to Harborview's seventh-floor ward. Irv Konopka suffered a fractured shoulder. Levi McCormack, who sustained a broken nose and cuts to the head and face, rested next to Ben Geraghty, who had a broken kneecap and a scalp laceration that required twenty-five stitches. Dick Powers sustained more significant injuries, including skull, neck, and back fractures. He was in a delirious state all night, shouting phrases like "Come on boy!" and "Bear down, Dick!" as if he was playing ball.[29]

Gus Hallbourg was initially nowhere to be found after the accident. It turned out that he had climbed up the mountain with some assistance and caught a ride back to Ellensburg, where he received treatment for cuts and burns to his right hand and both arms.[30]

Driver Glen Berg received treatment for severe burns to his face, neck, arms, and legs at Seattle's Virginia Mason Hospital. Investigators were anxious to question him about the crash, but he was in no shape to talk during the first forty-eight hours following the accident. In the meantime, police and reporters gathered the accounts of the less severely injured. From his hospital bed, McCormack lamented, "I don't know why we didn't smash the other driver. It might have been better."[31]

"I don't know why this had to happen to us," said Barisoff. "We were getting along swell. Now we're shot. Half the team's dead and the rest won't play for a long time. Poor ol' Konopka was signed to play pro football with the Detroit Lions this fall."[32]

Berg was finally able to give his account of the catastrophe to the King County coroner John Brill on June 27. Berg was unaware at the time that anyone had died in the accident. He mentioned the engine and brake trouble but said the cause of the crash was the oncoming car.[33]

Geraghty corroborated Berg's account: "I saw the lights coming. The car was on the wrong side. We either tried to miss it or skidded. I don't know. I went out a window too quick to tell."[34]

Mary Geraghty, accompanied by Joyce Collins, flew to Seattle to see her husband on the afternoon of June 25. "I told the children their praying saved you!" she exclaimed when she got to Ben's bedside. "They always pray for daddy to get hits and come home early."[35]

On the morning of June 26, Chris Hartje was still alive but in critical condition, 90 percent of his body burned.[36] Doctors gave him roughly twenty-five blood and plasma transfusions during the thirty-six hours following the accident.[37] His wife, Holly, seven months pregnant, was in San Francisco when the accident occurred. No one from the Indians called her, so she did not find out about the crash until someone called on the phone the next morning to ask if Chris was involved. She immediately ran down the street and picked up a newspaper, which confirmed the dreadful news.

Holly and her mother chartered a plane to Seattle later that day. The only aircraft available was an old cargo plane with a single bench seat. When they arrived in the Emerald City, they had no idea where to go. Holly got into a cab and explained the situation to the taxi driver, who knew the players were at Harborview. When they arrived at the hospital, Holly found her husband covered head to toe in bandages except for slits for his eyes and mouth. Because of his condition, she could neither hold his hand nor kiss him. The burns had damaged his nerve endings, so Chris felt no pain and did not realize the severity of his injuries. He told Holly, "Go get my clothes, I'm ready to get out of here."[38] Doctors then pulled Holly out of the room and explained that Chris was dying. He passed away on June 26 at 7:20 p.m., becoming the ninth fatality.

The loss of nine athletes in the prime of their lives was incomprehensible. Each had varying degrees of baseball promise, but all had bright futures and left behind devastated families, friends, and teammates. Besides Holly Hartje, the widows of Mel Cole and Freddie Martinez were also pregnant. Vic Picetti was engaged to be married. Bob Kinnaman and his girlfriend, Ruby Roberts, had planned to announce their engagement in the coming weeks.[39] One week after the crash, Kinnaman's father, Joe, died suddenly. He had been battling health problems for several years, and the shock of his son's death was thought to have been too much to bear.[40]

From the *Havre Daily News* to the *New York Times*, newspapers across the country ran Associated Press or United Press accounts of the tragedy, as did *The Sporting News* in its July 3 edition.

All Western International League games scheduled for June 25 were canceled. "The boys who died in the accident were probably some of the finest baseball prospects that have been seen in the Pacific Northwest," said Salem Senators business manager George Emigh, who mentioned that Cole was one of the "finest young men in baseball that I have known."[41]

The car that allegedly forced the bus off the road was never identified. A gas station attendant in Vantage, Washington, reported overhearing some customers talking about a car that sideswiped a bus the night of the crash. He gave authorities a license plate number but was unsure about the last digit.[42] A search for the vehicle came up empty.

Services for Vic Picetti were held on June 29 in San Francisco. The funeral home was so full of flowers that visitors paying their respects had a hard time squeezing in.[43] In the days and weeks that followed, the phone in the Picetti house rang incessantly with calls of condolences. Letters of sympathy filled the mailbox, including one from former St. Louis Browns scout Curtis Hammerbeck, who called Vic a great sportsman who was destined for the major leagues.[44]

Picetti's death shocked sportswriters and former teammates who had watched him mature from an amateur on the San Francisco sandlots to a polished professional with the Oakland Oaks. Cookie Devincenzi recalled that Picetti was regarded "like a son" during his time with the Oaks. "The boy had a brilliant future ahead of him," said Devincenzi. "Nearly all of the major-league clubs were after him. I had a call last fall from the Chicago

Cubs, who were seeking to buy him. Detroit, Boston Red Sox, and the Yankees were also interested in him."[45]

Bill Leiser, the reporter who traveled with Picetti to the *Esquire* All-American game in New York, wrote, "Unless the Oaks refused to sell for a reasonable price, Vic would have been property of Detroit before the year was out." Leiser pointed out that had Picetti signed with the highest bidder two years earlier, he would not have been on the Spokane bus. "His loyalty and purpose of mind were unusual for his years, as was his ability at first base." Leiser wrote that he "had long looked forward to the fun of watching [Picetti] climb to the top, as we all knew he would for sure."[46]

Richie Ashburn, who was playing in the Alaskan Army League, wrote an Omaha newspaper suggesting that Picetti be honored at the upcoming All-American game, where the pair had struck up a friendship two years earlier.[47] The 1946 game was held at Chicago's Wrigley Field on August 10 with Ty Cobb and Honus Wagner serving as managers. Picetti was remembered with a moment of silence during the pregame ceremony.

Vic was the apple of his mother's eye, and his death, just a year after the loss of her husband, was devastating. Angela eventually got a job at a consignment shop to make ends meet. She kept scrapbooks with Vic's baseball accomplishments and mementoes from his career for the rest of her life. Vic's sister, Beverly, married and moved to Bellingham, Washington. Robert Picetti, who was too young to remember Vic when he died, later recalled his mother becoming enraged any time she heard the name Casey Stengel—the man who sent her son to Spokane.[48]

Jack Lohrke stayed in Spokane for a day or so after the accident and then accompanied one of the grieving wives back to California. He stopped to see his parents in Los Angeles before making his way to San Diego, where he consoled Helen Martinez, the wife of his deceased roommate. When Lohrke reported to the Padres on June 30, owner Bill Starr bawled him out for taking so long. "Where have you been?" asked Starr. Lohrke replied, "I've been delivering widows."[49]

9

THE GAME MUST GO ON

Grief weighed heavy on Sam Collins, but he was a businessman determined to field a team as soon as possible. He believed "the boys themselves would want the game continued."[1] Two days after the accident, he met with league president Robert Abel in Spokane to map out a plan to rebuild the Indians roster and resume the season. Collins spent much of the day on the phone with Pacific Coast League teams trying to convince them to send a player or two to Spokane. Several Western International League teams, including the Salem Senators and Bremerton Bluejackets, offered to loan players to the Indians under the league's emergency rule. "We certainly would not want Mr. Collins to be forced into buying players he does not want, just in order to field a team again quickly," said Abel. "This tragic accident has struck all baseball, and all teams want to help."[2]

Calls poured into the sports desks of Spokane's two daily newspapers with offers of financial assistance for the survivors and families of the deceased players. The *Spokane Chronicle* sent telegrams to major league Commissioner Albert "Happy" Chandler and National Association of Professional Baseball Leagues president William Bramham, urging them to use their power to stage benefit games. In Spokane, community leaders formed a committee to manage a benefit fund. "I can't recall when anything has affected our entire population like this," said one committee member. "Each and every fan feels a deep personal loss. We have all wanted to be of assistance in some way and now we have our chance."[3]

After a series of phone calls, officials from the Seattle Rainiers and Oakland Oaks willingly agreed to play a benefit game at Ferris Field on July 8. The benefit committee set a goal of raising $50,000. Box seats cost $25 each, grandstand seats $5, and bleacher tickets $1.50.[4]

While arrangements for ballgames and fundraisers were being made in Spokane, funeral services were held for the nine departed ballplayers in their respective hometowns. Mel Cole received military honors at a funeral in Sacramento. His widow, Marianne, was in her third trimester of pregnancy and doctors would not clear her to travel. On September 16, she gave birth to a son named Melvin.

Five days after the accident, Ben Geraghty—his head still bandaged and his leg in a cast—signed a contract to manage the Indians through the 1947 season. Upon his discharge from Harborview Medical Center, he traveled back to Spokane and planned to start his new job. Geraghty and Pete Barisoff, both on crutches, attended the Indians' first practice at Ferris Field on June 30. The only other familiar faces were Milt Cadinha, Joe Faria, and trainer Dutch Anderson. New players from a variety of locales trickled in during the next couple of days. Infielder Lou Kubiak arrived on loan from Salem. The Indians signed former Victoria Athletics pitcher Al Raimondi, erstwhile Oakland infielder-outfielder Frank Hawkins, and ex–Washington State Cougar and Boston Braves farmhand Gale Bishop. Two other signees had been most recently toiling in the Mexican League and a couple were former pros playing semipro ball. A fellow named Bill Smith from Lake City, Iowa, had played some ball in the navy and hitchhiked west to Washington for a tryout. "I figured you might be needing some ballplayers," he said on his arrival.[5] Smith did not make the team.

After a couple of days at the helm, doctors ordered Geraghty to the sidelines. It turned out that he was in no condition to manage. In his place, Collins turned to Glenn Wright—the man he had fired at the start of the season. Wright still lived in Spokane and had gotten sober. Following only a handful of workouts, the new-look, makeshift Spokane Indians resumed play with an Independence Day doubleheader versus the Yakima Stars in front of 3,478 fans at Ferris Field. The Indians were still awaiting the arrival of some new players, so trainer Dutch Anderson filled in at third base. Cadinha started the first game and took the loss. Faria started the second contest and had the same fate as the Indians squandered an 8–1 lead. Though Anderson had never played professional baseball, he managed to hit a pair of doubles. Spokane proceeded to suffer defeats of 10–0, 12–7, and 24–1 before Cadinha finally put the remade Indians in the win column with a two-hit shutout on July 7.

Ticket sales were initially slow for the Oaks-Rainiers benefit game on July 8. Bing Crosby, who played baseball at Gonzaga University, bought $2,500 worth of tickets, which he donated to service personnel. A local cab company owner made sure no one missed the game because of a lack of transportation, offering free rides to anyone who needed a lift.[6] The pace of sales ultimately ticked up, but steady rain on game day kept some folks away. An estimated 5,500 fans—men dressed in sport coats, ties, and fedoras and women in jackets and scarves—filed into Ferris Field for the somber event. Nine empty seats behind home plate were covered in flowers to honor the fallen ballplayers. In the memorial program that sold for $1, Dave Kirk of the *Spokane Chronicle* wrote, "I am the shadow sinister called Fate, by whose whimsy you are here tonight. Without my sanction, no man moves, or conquers, or dies. . . . I am the Master Umpire and I call the plays the way I see them. I have raised my arm, and nine grand boys are out."[7]

At 7:15 p.m., the Spokane American Legion band performed the "Star-Spangled Banner." Father Arthur Dussault, a Jesuit priest from Gonzaga University, opened the pregame ceremony with a prayer that concluded: "In loving and reverent memory, we who have [been] left behind dedicate solemnly tonight's game to those members of Spokane's 1946 baseball team who will live forever in our hearts. Eternal rest grant unto them, O Lord. And let perpetual light shine upon them. May they rest in peace. Amen."[8] Spokane mayor Arthur Meehan spoke briefly after a bugler played "Taps." Johnny Price, a skilled baseball entertainer, lightened the mood with a thirty-minute pregame show. His feats included catching fly balls in his hip pockets, fielding balls while standing on his head, and hitting baseballs while hanging upside down. Vic Picetti's former Oaks' teammates, piloted by Casey Stengel, defeated the Rainiers, 5–3, in a rain-shortened game.

The Indians finished July with a 10–20 record. Unless Cadinha or Faria pitched, the team had virtually no chance of winning. When they did pitch, Spokane usually lost due to a lack of offense. In one game against Victoria,

Faria took a no-hitter into the seventh inning, but ultimately lost, 1–0. The pre-tragedy iteration of the Indians had destroyed Victoria pitching game after game. Besides enduring numerous on-field defeats, Cadinha and Faria played with the constant thought of their departed teammates. "I guess that's the way the good Lord wanted it," said Cadinha, looking back, "but every game we played and every town we traveled to, we had the players on our minds."[9]

Though countless teams in professional baseball sent Collins telegrams offering to loan the Indians players in the immediate aftermath of the bus crash, few acted on the promise. "Brooklyn and the St. Louis Browns were the only clubs to back up their offers with players," lamented Collins. "Every Coast League team promised players, but all they gave me were castoffs."[10] As a result, Spokane's manpower and talent shortage continued throughout the summer, prompting business manager Dwight Aden to dust off his Indians uniform and play outfield for a few games. Only one of the bus crash survivors made it back to the field that season; Gus Hallbourg rejoined the Indians on July 30. The ten runs he gave up to Victoria in his first outing were perhaps an indication he returned too soon.

Branch Rickey visited Spokane in late July and made a bid to buy the Indians or, at minimum, secure an affiliation with his Brooklyn Dodgers. Rickey had been putting out feelers to purchase the Indians even before the bus accident.[11] The Dodgers had only one minor league team out west, a Class C team in Santa Barbara, California, and they sought to expand their footprint. To garner some goodwill, Rickey had already agreed to send two players to help Spokane get through the rest of the season. Collins did not want to relinquish his team entirely, but after a series of meetings with Rickey he reached an agreement for Spokane to become a Dodgers affiliate through the 1947 season. Collins cited the difficulty he had filling a roster after the crash as the impetus for linking up.[12] The Dodgers allowed Geraghty to return as manager in 1947 and have ultimate say on which players made the roster. Players selected by Spokane in the spring would remain with the club through the end of the season.[13] The pact benefitted both sides but would not help the Indians' severe talent shortage in the remaining weeks of the 1946 season.

Though the Indians had received little in the way of manpower assistance, generous monetary donations for the benefit fund poured in from across the country. Many came as a result of fundraising games played by American Legion, semipro, and minor league teams. A check for $4,605.05 came from Reno, Nevada, where bartenders and gamblers staged a benefit softball game. Bob Hope mailed a check for $500. A junior softball team from New Orleans sent $5, a barbershop in Indiana donated $2.[14] In Spokane, organizers held a charity hole-in-one contest in which half of the proceeds went to the benefit fund.[15] The event, staged downtown at Monroe and Mallon, took place over the course of sixteen days, with 34,215 shots attempted. A fellow named Curt Bolton scored the first hole-in-one and took home a Stinson airplane valued at $6,000. Additional prizes included a trip to New York, a new car, and a refrigerator. The event raised more than $11,000.[16] Ferris Field concessionaire Al Williams wrote letters to all 350 professional baseball teams and offered to sell copies of the Indians' memorial program. Nearly three hundred teams responded, including one that ordered fifty copies. Williams received more than $1,000 through his efforts, pushing the benefit fund to near $87,000.[17]

In the dog days of August, some of the Indians' replacement players more or less threw in the towel. One infielder refused to play the back end of a Sunday doubleheader, resulting in a suspension. Some players got into the habit of showing up ten minutes before game time, as if they were playing for a recreation league team. Others refused to play because of mild injuries. As a result, trainer Dutch Anderson played third base regularly, and pitchers Cadinha, Faria, and Hallbourg often roamed the outfield when they were not on the mound. "There isn't a fellow in town who will be happier than Collins when the curtain finally rings down on the Western International campaign," wrote Bob Johnson in the *Spokane Chronicle*.[18]

Cadinha performed yeoman's work following the accident and ended the season with twenty-three complete games and 233 innings pitched. On nights when he started, attendance figures doubled. The righty, who had a pre-crash win-loss record of 8–1, ended the campaign with a 16–7 mark and 3.55 ERA. Had it not been for the accident, he might have won twenty easily. At the conclusion of the season, the Hollywood Stars of the PCL purchased Cadinha's contract for $5,000.[19] Faria, Spokane's other workhorse, pitched 183 innings while registering a 7–12 record. Hallbourg ended the season with a 7–6 ledger and 6.75 ERA.

The Indians lost twelve of their last thirteen games to finish the season 54–78, good for seventh place, ahead of only Victoria. The Wenatchee Chiefs vaulted past the Salem Senators in late July and won the league pennant with a record of 89–54. The Indians had been eight games above .500 when the crash occurred and were thirty below after. They would have undoubtedly been in contention for the league title had the club remained intact. Johnson was even more bullish. "There isn't a fan in Spokane who isn't convinced that the old team would have won the Willy pennant by 10 games," he opined. "There wasn't a club in the league with the polish, the will to win and the ability to compare with that team which met death at Snoqualmie Pass."[20]

Donations to the benefit fund continued to arrive through the end of the season. The fund ultimately totaled more than $118,000—the equivalent of more than $1.8 million in 2023 dollars. After subtracting roughly $4,000 to cover expenses and taxes, the money was dispersed to fifteen recipients during the winter. "After many meetings and extensive investigation, the committee divided the beneficiaries into five classifications," described the *Spokane Chronicle*.[21] Dick Powers, who had teetered on the edge of death for weeks after the accident and spent months in a head-to-waist cast, received the largest payout.[22] Widows with children were given the next highest priority. The five survivors besides Powers received the smallest amounts. Bus driver Glen Berg, who had a lengthy recovery from severe burns, did not receive any of the benefit money.

The widows and families of several players filed claims against the Washington Motor Coach Company for damages alleged to have been caused by negligence. Sam Collins was appointed administrator of the estates of Chris Hartje, Bob James, Bob Paterson, George Lyden, George Risk, and Freddie Martinez in Spokane County Superior Court. The bus company denied any negligence on its part or the part of Glen Berg but made settlement offers in each case. The parents of Bob James received $5,000 and the widows of the other five players settled for between $12,000 and $20,000.[23] In a San Francisco court, Angela Picetti was awarded a settlement of $27,500.[24]

Jack Lohrke did not receive the warmest of welcomes in San Diego. The Padres' third baseman, former Boston Brave, and longtime Seattle Indians/Rainiers star Dick Gyselman greeted him by saying, "I don't know where you're playing son, but I'm playing third base."[25] Instead of the hot corner, manager Pepper Martin installed Lohrke at shortstop. "Martin was from the old school," recalled Lohrke. "He just wanted you to hustle."[26] That was no problem for Jack.

Lohrke debuted with the Padres on June 30 and hit .467 (fourteen for thirty) with a home run and four doubles in his first ten games.[27] While tearing up PCL pitching, Lohrke quickly acquired a fitting nickname that rolled off the tongue: Lucky Lohrke. It became a moniker that would stick with him for the rest of his life, though he was never comfortable with it. It was, after all, a constant reminder of his fallen brothers in the military and baseball who had not been as fortunate.

Lohrke finished the PCL season with a .303 average, eight home runs, and forty-eight RBIs. Five-time major league All-Star Lon Warnecke, now an umpire in the PCL, called Lohrke the best player in the circuit.[28]

"He should become one of baseball's all-time stars," assessed Martin. "He has the proper attitude, worlds of natural ability, and plenty of fortitude."[29]

The Padres were inundated with offers from major league teams who sought Lohrke's services for the 1947 season. The Boston Braves outbid six competing teams with an offer of cash, outfielder Johnny Barrett, and three players on option. The *San Diego Union* reported at the time that the Padres would have received $7,500.[30] Years later, Padres owner Bill Starr told the *Los Angeles Times* that the deal would have netted his team $50,000.[31]

The news of Lohrke's big league advance thrilled his supporters in Spokane. "There isn't a fan amongst us who won't stand up and holler that it couldn't have happened to a finer fellow," wrote Bob Johnson in the *Spokane Chronicle*.[32]

Lohrke would never suit up in Beantown, however. Because the Braves had not obtained waivers on three players involved in the transaction before a specified deadline, Commissioner Happy Chandler nixed the deal. Starr later called the snafu one of the saddest experiences of his baseball career.[33] The New York Giants jumped at the opportunity to pick Lohrke in the Rule 5 draft at a price of $10,000.[34] "When the Giants took him, I was devastated," said Starr in 1990. "We would have gotten three very important players, plus some very important money, and the Braves had said they guaranteed delivery. I think they could have gotten waivers in time, or if they couldn't, that they could have adjusted the deal somehow."[35] Starr took heat in the press for letting Lohrke get away for such a paltry return.

Now, Lohrke, like Vic Picetti two years earlier in the *Esquire* All-American game, would play for manager Mel Ott at the Polo Grounds.

10

THE YEAR AFTER

"I was the oldest guy on that bus. Why did I live instead of those kids?"[1] Ben Geraghty pondered that question often. He believed he was saved for some purpose and would spend the rest of his life feeling like he was on borrowed time, in search of the reason for his second chance.[2]

By the spring of 1947, Geraghty's scalp and busted kneecap had healed. He still experienced occasional headaches, but eight months after climbing out of the ravine, he was eager to get to work as manager of the Spokane Indians.[3] Following an offseason of convalescence at his East Coast home, Geraghty drove his family across the country to Spokane before turning around and making a five-day journey from Washington State to Pensacola, Florida, where the Brooklyn Dodgers held a novel minor league spring training school. Branch Rickey's focus on player development manifested in a dawn-to-dusk program in which two hundred prospects practiced all day and attended evening lectures that stretched past midnight.

While Brooklyn's farmhands learned the finer points of baseball in the Florida panhandle, Leo Durocher's big league Dodgers trained in Havana, Cuba. Rickey had moved major league camp to the island nation after Jackie Robinson faced threats, taunts, and segregation in the Jim Crow South the previous spring. Besides Robinson, Brooklyn had signed three more Black players: Roy Campanella, Roy Partlow, and Don Newcombe. Robinson would make Brooklyn's opening day roster and break baseball's color barrier on April 15, but Durocher wouldn't be there to see it. Days before Robinson's historic debut, Commissioner Happy Chandler suspended

Durocher for the entire 1947 season because of his public affair with married actress Laraine Day and associations with gamblers and gangsters.

Geraghty spent a few weeks in Florida then traveled to San Bernardino, California, where his Spokane Indians held a joint training camp with the Dodgers' Santa Barbara affiliate. With the exception of Levi McCormack, the Indians' new-look roster was filled with young players who had advanced from the Dodgers' Class C and D teams. McCormack, thirty-three, resumed his baseball career for what would be his fifth season in Spokane. One scribe quipped that the veteran outfielder had played so long at Ferris Field that he could claim squatter's rights.[4]

A sore shoulder limited McCormack to sixteen at-bats in the Indians' first twenty-five regular season games, but he quickly returned to his customary form. By June 18, he was hitting .299 with twenty-five RBIs. In late July, the Indians honored him with a "McCormack Night" promotion that attracted a crowd of nearly eight thousand. Spokane's beloved ballplayer received a plaque from league president Robert Abel and numerous gifts, including a new Buick Roadmaster, golf balls, and a set of luggage. Though he was slowed by a sore hip related to the bus accident, McCormack ended the season hitting .276 with seventy-six RBIs, a productive showing that earned him a spot in the Western International League All-Star game.

Geraghty appeared in thirty-one games and hit .348 while piloting the 1947 Indians to contention for the WIL title. However, he nearly lost his job early in the season because of a falling out with Sam Collins and Rickey over the team's release of outfielder Len Scarpelli, who was hitting .313 at the time. Geraghty's gripes to the local papers angered his bosses but his winning record kept him employed. The Indians finished twenty games over .500, a half-game behind the first-place Vancouver Capilanos.

After the season concluded, Collins sold the team to former minor league player-manager John "Buddy" Ryan and attorney J. Lamar Butler. Collins delivered parting shots at Geraghty, criticizing his coaching ability while declaring that the Indians would have won ten more games under another manager. Bob Johnson of the *Spokane Chronicle* challenged Collins's claims, opining that Geraghty "had his ballplayers behind him 100 percent" and performed brilliantly. "The team lined up behind Ben and had nothing but a good word for him," wrote Johnson. "What they had to say about the ownership doesn't come under the heading of 'family reading.'"[5]

Levi McCormack had established roots in Spokane, but his status with the Indians remained in limbo as the 1948 season approached. Ryan and Butler invited him to try out with the team but were noncommittal when it came to a contract. "We are not running any popularity contests," said Butler. "Any man who wants to try out for the Indians can do so, and welcome. If he wears the suit, he will have made the team on his ability."[6] The owners' brush-off of the local legend would result in the end of his professional baseball career. McCormack finished with a .308 batting average and thirty-one home runs in eight minor league seasons. He played in the Spokane semipro circuit for the next couple of years and ultimately found employment with the US Postal Service as a mail carrier. Levi and his wife, Margaret, raised three boys and four girls. McCormack remained a staple in the community until he died suddenly of a heart attack in 1974 at age sixty-one. After his death, former teammate Edo Vanni described the internal scars his friend carried following the 1946 tragedy: "He never got over the shock and frustration of lying there, helpless, and watching the flames consume his best friends."[7]

Three of the other four crash survivors returned to the field in 1947. Irv Konopka signed with the Boise Pilots of the Class C Pioneer League but quit after ten games. Though his fractured shoulder had healed, the residual effects left him unable to throw. The injury also ended his professional football aspirations. Konopka subsequently moved back to Wisconsin, where he taught high school English and worked construction jobs during summers. For reasons unknown, Konopka changed his last name to Kane in the late 1950s. He died of cancer in 1968 at age forty-eight.

Pete Barisoff finally made it to Bremerton as a member of the 1947 Bluejackets, teaming up with his brother, Bill, who was coming off a league-leading forty home run season. Pete pitched in seventeen games, registering a 5–4 record and 5.34 ERA before abruptly leaving the team in early August. He next resurfaced in professional baseball two years later with the San Bernardino Pioneers. In a cruel twist of fate, Barisoff died of smoke inhalation in a house fire on November 12, 1949, after apparently falling asleep with a lit cigarette. His wife Shirley and two sons were not home at the time. Barisoff was only twenty-four. He is remembered as a hero for saving Konopka's life immediately after the bus crash.

Gus Hallbourg had the longest professional playing career of the crash survivors, pitching two more seasons for a Class B team called the Red Roses in Lancaster, Pennsylvania. He compiled a 15–21 record with earned run averages above 4.00 in each campaign. After the 1948 season, he moved to Stockton, California, and took a job with Pacific Telephone, his employer for the next thirty-three years. He and his wife, Roberta, settled in Manteca, California, where they raised their four children.

Milt Cadinha and Joe Faria, forever linked because of a fateful convertible ride, had eerily similar ends to their pitching careers. Cadinha returned home to Northern California after the 1946 season and looked forward to twirling in the Pacific Coast League for the Hollywood Stars in 1947. During a semipro game that winter, he experimented with a screwball and felt a sudden flash of pain in his right arm, the result of a fractured bone near the elbow.[8] Because of the injury, his sale to Hollywood was nullified and he remained property of the Spokane Indians. Cadinha did not pitch in 1947 and was sold to Fort Worth in the Texas League following the season. He reportedly suffered a back injury days before he was scheduled to depart for Texas the following spring.[9] By April 1948, Cadinha was back to playing semipro ball in California but never did report to Fort Worth. He pitched on Bay Area semipro teams for the next several years and went to work in the insurance business. Milt and his wife, Yuvonna, had two children.

Joe Faria went to spring training with the Oakland Oaks in 1947. His tryout included three shutout innings against the Chicago Cubs, an outing that helped earn him a spot in Casey Stengel's bullpen. In one contest early in the season against the San Diego Padres, Faria came on in relief. While delivering one particular pitch, he felt a pop in his right arm. "I felt my arm go limp," he later recalled. "I had chipped a bone in my right elbow. . . . I was washed up at 28."[10] The Oaks released Faria a few days later. Like his pal Milt, Joe pitched on semipro teams but never played professional baseball again. Fortuitously, a few months before the injury, Faria had purchased a vacant lot on Fourteenth Street in San Leandro, just south of Oakland. When it was clear his pitching career was over, he began construction on a bar and restaurant he named the Stadium Club. It opened in the fall of 1947 and remained in business for thirty-seven years, serving as popular hangout for baseball celebrities. In the 1980s, Faria catered team dinners to the Oakland Athletics clubhouse.

Of the six players who survived the bus crash, Dick Powers was the only one who never again played professionally. He had a steel plate placed in his head and spent nearly a year lying on his back in a body cast recuperating from his spinal fractures at Oakland's Merritt Hospital. Later, he would recall how maggots were used to eat dead skin under the cast as a means of preventing infection.[11] During his recovery, Powers received letters from well-wishers across the country. In December 1946, he wrote a letter to the Spokane American Legion Post expressing his appreciation for the monetary donation and support: "It makes me feel good to know there are so many nice people in the world. I'm sorry that I cannot play for the swell people of Spokane who are really loyal baseball fans, but I know that now I will never be a successful baseball pitcher."[12]

A silver lining of Powers's prolonged hospitalization was getting to know a young candy striper named Edith Hunt. The pair hit it off and married soon after Dick was discharged. Though his dreams of a career in baseball were dashed, Powers made a remarkable recovery and actually pitched in semipro games in 1948. He exhibited no lingering effects from his injuries and kept physically active throughout his life. He and Edith had six children: Joanna, Richard Jr., Thomas, James, Patricia, and Michael. Powers built his family's Oakland Hills home on a steep plot of land, constructed steps in the yard out of railroad ties, and did all of his own painting and landscaping. He had careers in the wholesale meat business and later in real estate. When his kids were growing up, Powers coached a youth team sponsored by Hoffmeyer Belting and a Babe Ruth League team called the Rockridge Lions. He and his family regularly exercised at an Oakland athletic club, where they swam and played basketball and handball. Dick and Edith divorced in 1968; three years later, Dick remarried a schoolteacher named Diana Vallance. Later in life, Powers enjoyed golf, classic movies, and Breyer's mint chocolate chip ice cream. One of his granddaughters recalled that he always seemed grumpy. She was told that it was because his dream of becoming a pro ball player was taken from him when his career was just heating up.[13]

Once Glen Berg recovered from his injuries, he returned to work and spent decades driving delivery trucks, surpassing a million miles on the road without so much as a fender bender. "Co-workers were struck by his extraordinary reliability, his passion for safety, his willingness to serve as a mentor to younger drivers," wrote Jim Price in the *Spokesman-Review*.[14] Berg was described as kind, reliable, and intensely private. He had a reputation as someone who would always lend a hand at the drop of a hat. He attended church regularly, sang in the choir, and occasionally drove the church bus. Berg taught both of his daughters how to play ball, but he never went to Spokane Indians games and never spoke of the crash. He died in 2003 at the age of eighty-one.

The playing careers of Jack Lohrke's surviving Spokane Indians teammates were fleeting, but his was just getting started. On Valentine's Day in 1947, the Pasadena Junior College varsity baseball team squared off against a team of alumni. Jackie Robinson, who was on the precipice of breaking baseball's color barrier, played second base for the alumni team; Lohrke manned the hot corner. Both players were about to leave for spring training to compete for infield jobs with New York clubs; Robinson with the Dodgers and Lohrke with the Giants. The day after the exhibition, Lohrke departed for Giants camp in Phoenix, Arizona.

Lohrke had stayed sharp during the winter playing ball with Vince DiMaggio and future brother-in-law Nick Sunseri on a Hermosa Beach semipro team sponsored by the United Aircraft Workers. He arrived at camp in midseason form, primed to compete for the Giants' open third-base job. His competition included incumbent Bill Rigney, veteran Sid Gordon, and fellow rookie Bobby Thomson. Lohrke's hustle made a strong first impression on regulars, rookies, and—most importantly—team brass.

Lon Warnecke, the former major league star who recommended Lohrke to the Giants, remained bullish on the young infielder. "He seems to have everything," gushed Warnecke to the *New York Times*. "He's a great competitor, has a good arm and a great pair of hands, and is fast. He'll hit many a two-bagger and drive in those runs. He's not a long-ball hitter, but he'll use that stick well enough. He's the best rookie prospect I've seen in fifteen years. . . . His timing on ground balls is wonderful. He plays the ball, doesn't let the ball play him."[15]

During spring training, sportswriters noticed something unusual about Lohrke; he wore a red flannel shirt underneath his Giants jersey. When asked about the mismatched garment, he reluctantly admitted that it was a shirt he took with him when he departed the bus in Ellensburg. "I wouldn't feel right without it," Lohrke said, "I got to wear it."[16]

Lohrke made the Giants' opening day roster and was about to see a lifelong dream come true. Mel Ott moved Thomson and Gordon to the outfield and Rigney to second base to accommodate Jack's slick glove and strong throwing arm at the hot corner. Lohrke made his debut on April 18 in the Giants' home opener versus the Dodgers at the Polo Grounds. A crowd of 38,736 filed through the turnstiles. Under clouded skies, Lohrke stepped into a major league batter's box for the first time. Less than three years earlier, Vic Picetti experienced a similar thrill at the Polo Grounds. Like Picetti's matchup against Blly Pierce, Lohrke faced a tough lefty in the form of Vic Lombardi, who was unbeaten in nine decisions against the Giants in the two previous seasons. And like Picetti, Lohrke delivered a base hit in his first at-bat, pulling a single to left field. When the Dodgers came to bat in the next inning, Robinson—who had debuted three days earlier—clubbed his first career home run into the left-field grandstand. Later, he singled to start a two-run rally. Robinson's standout performance was not enough to overcome six home runs by the Giants, who clobbered their rivals, 10–4.

Lohrke started the next six contests, recording three singles in his first twenty at-bats. The Giants had lost seven of nine to that point, and Ott, looking for an offensive spark, benched Lohrke in favor of Rigney. Lohrke played sparingly in May and the first three weeks of June. In one of his rare opportunities, he blasted the first home run of his big league career in a Giants' 13–10 home win over the Pittsburgh Pirates. Lohrke was inserted back in the starting lineup on June 21 and his bat got hot. He entrenched himself at the number eight spot in Ott's formidable batting order for the remainder of the season. Lohrke was part of a talented Giants rookie class that included Thomson, Clint Hartung, and twenty-one-game winner Larry Jansen. Another up-and-comer, outfielder Whitey Lockman, missed most of season because of a broken leg.

The Giants lineup boasted extraordinary power hitting led by first baseman Johnny Mize (fifty-one home runs), catcher Walker Cooper (thirty-five), and outfielder Willard Marshall (thirty-six)—each of whom topped the one hundred RBI mark. Thomson added twenty-nine homers, and three other players, including Lohrke, were in double figures. Ott's Giants hit so many homers that Marshall's round-tripper on August 31 put them in a tie with the 1936 Yankees for the single-season home run record with 182. The next day, Lohrke delivered the record-breaking blast off Boston Braves reliever Red Barrett, which proved to be the decisive blow in the Giants' 2–1 victory.

On September 9, Lohrke hit another game-winning home run—a two-run shot off Preacher Roe at Pittsburgh's Forbes Field to break a 1–1 tie. Jack would later recall another thrill in the Steel City—meeting Hall of Fame shortstop Honus Wagner. Lohrke concluded the season with a .240 average, eleven home runs, and thirty-five RBIs for the fourth-place Giants (81–73), who finished thirteen games back of Brooklyn. Jackie Robinson's .297 average, twelve home runs, and twenty-nine stolen bases earned him the National League Rookie of the Year Award.

Lohrke, a defensive stalwart, was charged with an uncharacteristic twenty errors during his rookie season. Decades later, Lockman and Lohrke shared a laugh when recollecting the reason for the surprisingly high number of miscues. Mize, the first baseman, could not handle a lot of Lohrke's rockets from across the diamond, and official scorers were more apt to charge errors to the rookie than to the veteran.[17]

Lohrke achieved his dream of playing in the major leagues. In many ways, he was representing Vic Picetti, Freddie Martinez, Bob Kinnaman, and Bob Paterson—players who possessed big-league ability but never got the chance.

Players line up in the dugout of the Polo Grounds in New York at the Esquire All-American game on August 7, 1944. Vic Picetti is fourth from left. Also pictured are Hall of Famers Richie Ashburn (far left), Mel Ott, and Carl Hubbell (fifth and sixth from left, respectively). *Courtesy Lesley Thorgeirson*

Dolph Camilli and Vic Picetti with the Oakland Oaks in 1945. Picetti turned down big league contracts to play for his idol and fellow San Franciscan. *Courtesy David Eskenazi*

Levi McCormack with the Spokane Indians in 1939. *Courtesy David Eskenazi*

Bob Kinnaman won twenty-two games for the Spokane Indians in 1941 before enlisting in the army during World War II. *Courtesy David Eskenazi*

Facing page top: Edo Vanni, Danny Escobar, Levi McCormack, and Bob Kinnaman at the Naval Recruiting Station in Seattle in 1942. The navy rejected Kinnaman because he had teeth knocked out from a line drive, so he joined the army. *Courtesy Lisa Johnson*

Facing page bottom: Vic Picetti receives instruction from Casey Stengel during Oakland Oaks spring training in 1946. Oakland's roster was full of returning war veterans, so Stengel ultimately sent Picetti to Spokane to get regular playing time. *Courtesy Caren Sutton*

U.S. NAVY
U.S. NAVY
Let's make all batting averages high against America's Enemies. Navy Rec. Sta. Seattle.

Mel Cole with the Wenatchee Chiefs in 1939. *Courtesy David Eskenazi*

Idaho Falls Russets team photo, 1941. Bob James is in the top row, far right. *Courtesy Alicia Hicks*

Before Chris Hartje got his cup of coffee with the Brooklyn Dodgers, he caught for the Kansas City Blues—the New York Yankees' top farm team. *Courtesy Caren Sutton*

Chris Hartje blocks the plate during a game with the Syracuse Chiefs. Hartje spent parts of three seasons with Syracuse before serving in the coast guard during World War II. *Courtesy Caren Sutton*

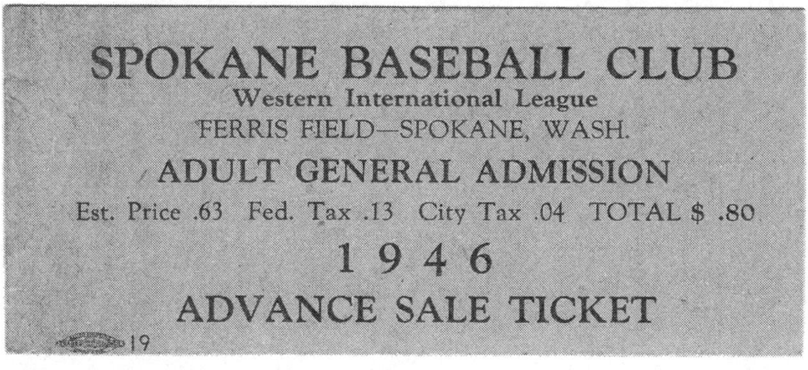

Spokane Indians ticket stub from 1946. *Courtesy David Eskenazi*

Bob Paterson, shown here during the 1946 season wearing a catcher's mitt, roamed center field for the Spokane Indians. *Courtesy Lesley Thorgeirson*

First baseman Vic Picetti with the Spokane Indians during the 1946 season. *Courtesy Lesley Thorgeirson*

Spokane Indians team photo taken on June 22, 1946—two days before the tragic bus crash. Back row, left to right: Dwight Aden, Chris Hartje, Vic Picetti, Pete Barisoff, George Risk, Dick Powers, Ben Geraghty, Gus Hallbourg, Milt Cadinha, Mel Cole, and John "Dutch" Anderson. Front row: Joe Faria, George Lyden, Irv Konopka, Bob Paterson, Bob Kinnaman, Levi McCormack, Jack Lohrke, Fred Martinez, and Bob James. Seated: Batboy Kenny Benshoof. *Courtesy David Eskenazi*

San Diego Padres manager Pepper Martin with Jack Lohrke in the summer of 1946. *Courtesy David Eskenazi*

Joe Faria, Pete Barisoff, Ben Geraghty, and Milt Cadinha at Ferris Field in July 1946 as the Spokane Indians reorganize following the crash. *Courtesy David Eskenazi*

Cover of the memorial program sold at the Oakland Oaks–Seattle Rainiers benefit game on July 8, 1946, at Ferris Field in Spokane. *Courtesy David Eskenazi*

Henry Aaron and Ben Geraghty with the Jacksonville Braves in 1953. *Courtesy Scott Kornberg/Jacksonville Shrimp*

Ben Geraghty is honored during a pregame ceremony with the Louisville Colonels in 1960. *Courtesy Eric Vickrey*

Jack Lohrke spent seven seasons in the major leagues and then played several years in the Pacific Coast League, including two with the Seattle Rainiers. *Courtesy David Eskenazi*

11

THE ULTIMATE BASEBALL MAN

The finest human being I have ever known is Ben Geraghty.

—Henry Aaron[1]

Ben Geraghty was stuck in a catch-22. He wanted to manage in the major leagues but to achieve that goal, he needed to gain experience in the minor leagues. And that meant riding buses. Road trips that had once been a routine part of his job were now a test of will.

One bit of solace for Geraghty in 1948 was the fact that he no longer had to travel over Snoqualmie Pass. The Spokane Indians' new owners invited him to return despite Sam Collins's critical remarks in the press, but Geraghty instead accepted a more lucrative deal to manage a Cleveland farm team in Meridian, Mississippi. His tenure in Spokane was over after an eventful year and a half.

The 1948 season didn't go as Geraghty planned. The Class B Meridian Peps lacked talent and by the end of May were mired in last place. Geraghty stepped down after only two months on the job "for the good of the team."[2] A month later, he accepted a managerial job with the Class D Palatka Azaleas in the Florida State League, where he finished out the season.

Geraghty spent the winter coaching basketball at Seton Hall College and St. Benedict's Preparatory School in Newark, then turned his attention back to baseball in the spring of 1949, landing a post with a New York

Giants affiliate in Bristol, Virginia. Known as the Twins because the town stretched across the Virginia-Tennessee state line, the team played in the Class D Appalachian League—as far removed from the major leagues as a professional ball club could be.

Geraghty, now thirty-six, had served the dual role of player-manager in Spokane and Meridian, but he still experienced lingering effects of the knee injury he sustained in the bus crash.[3] In Bristol, he preferred to let the prospects play and step in only as a last resort. As it turned out, Geraghty did not need to test his gimpy knee. The Twins posted a 76–41 record and advanced to the league championship. Geraghty's "shrewd, skillful handling of players and sound knowledge of the art of baseball" did not go unnoticed.[4] Giants scout Bob Martin called him "one of the best judges and handlers of young players in the organization."[5]

Geraghty possessed an uncanny ability to evaluate players quickly and accurately. If he judged that a youngster lacked the necessary tools to advance, he would not hesitate to send him packing. His decision making was so swift that sportswriters gave him nicknames such as "Hatchet Man" and "Wood Chopper."[6] But if Geraghty saw glimpses of talent, he had a knack for helping players maximize their abilities. "And he doesn't appear to ever miss," observed one New Jersey scribe.[7] "Whatever you did for Geraghty, it was your potential fulfilled," wrote minor league pitcher and author Pat Jordan.[8]

Geraghty's handling of spring training in Sanford, Florida, in his second year with Bristol exemplified his winning mentality. Fearing he would lose players to the Giants' Class B or C affiliates if his team performed too well in meaningless exhibition games, he reported some players sick and kept some of his better players out of the starting lineup. The tactic assured that his preferred players would head north with him.[9] Geraghty's strategy paid dividends; the Twins won more than 60 percent of their games for a second straight year.

Geraghty's success in Bristol earned him a promotion within the Giants' minor league system heading into the 1951 campaign. He would now pilot the Class A Jacksonville Tars of the South Atlantic League—commonly known as the Sally League. Though he spent only two seasons in Bristol, Geraghty left an indelible mark. "He will long be remembered for his gambling style of play which has produced many wins when the game seemed hopelessly lost," wrote the *Bristol Herald Courier*.[10]

Geraghty inherited a Jacksonville team that was coming off a last-place season and had not captured a Sally League pennant in more than two decades. The Tars faced an early acid test in a spring training contest versus the mighty Boston Red Sox on April 4. Boston, heavy favorites to win the American League pennant, rolled out a star-studded lineup that included three future Hall of Famers—Ted Williams, Lou Boudreau, and Bobby Doerr—plus stalwarts Dom DiMaggio, Johnny Pesky, and Vern Stephens. Geraghty always managed with a high level of anxiety, but facing the fearsome Red Sox caused his nervousness to rachet up a notch. He chain-smoked in an attempt to calm his nerves, failing to notice that falling ashes from his cigarettes burned multiple holes in his pants and shirt.[11] Somehow, Geraghty's band of novices found a way to defeat the Red Sox, 8–7. Momentum from the stunning upset carried into the regular season. Jacksonville finished in second place and lost to the Montgomery Rebels in the league championship.

The Tars fell off in Geraghty's second year, finishing sixteen games below .500 and seventh out of eight teams. After the season, the New York Giants' agreement with the Jacksonville franchise expired and the Tars ownership changed hands. Despite the shakeup, Geraghty agreed to remain as manager, even though it would be under the umbrella of a different organization. Within a few weeks, Jacksonville became an affiliate of the Boston Braves, and the team name changed from Tars to Braves. The big league iteration of the Braves was not long for Beantown, however. Owner Lou Perini relocated the franchise to Milwaukee that spring. As manager of the Jacksonville Braves in 1953, Geraghty would face a new set of challenges that had nothing to do with baseball.

Though Jackie Robinson had broken the major league color barrier six years earlier, Jim Crow practices in the South had prevented Black players from playing in most minor leagues below the Mason-Dixon line in the years since. Robinson himself was barred from playing in Jacksonville during the spring of 1947. City officials, who disdained the idea of Black and White players sharing the same field, padlocked the stadium and stationed police outside in order to prevent Robinson and his teammates from playing a scheduled exhibition game. Six years later, there still had not been a player of color in the forty-nine-year existence of the Sally League—a circuit with teams in South Carolina, Georgia, Alabama, and Florida. That was about to change.

The Milwaukee Braves had several Black players under contract who needed minor league assignments for the 1953 season, including a highly touted nineteen-year-old named Henry Aaron. After the Braves purchased his contract from the Negro American League's Indianapolis Clowns the previous summer, the youngster from Mobile, Alabama, hit .336 and won his league's Rookie of the Year Award with the Class C Eau Claire Bears. Though Aaron may not have been quite ready for the major leagues, he was certainly ready for a higher level of competition. He, along with hundreds of other players from the Braves' minor league ranks, attended spring training in Waycross, Georgia, under the watchful eye of Geraghty and his fellow minor league managers. At the end of camp, Aaron and two other players of color—Horace Garner and Puerto Rican Félix Mantilla—were assigned to Jacksonville. The three Braves farmhands, along with Fleming Reedy and Al Israel of the Savannah Indians, would integrate the Sally League. Geraghty sat down with his three Black players at the start of the season and let them know what challenges they could expect in the Deep South. "It was nothing we didn't already know," recalled Aaron years later, "but it was reassuring to hear that the manager was on our side."[12]

To Aaron, Geraghty didn't look or act the part of a typical manager. "He was a small guy, with a long chin and hound-dog eyes—and he didn't speak the King's English," wrote Aaron in his autobiography *I Had a Hammer*. Aaron noticed that Geraghty carried an inordinate amount of anxiety, drank too much, and often arrived at the ballpark looking disheveled, sometimes wearing the same clothes he had worn the day before. Though Geraghty had his shortcomings, his baseball acumen and instincts were unmatched. "In all the years I played baseball, I never had a manager who cared more for his players or knew more about the game," recalled Aaron.[13]

Geraghty used alcohol to cope with bus travel and remained haunted by the Snoqualmie Pass crash, but to achieve his goal of managing in the major leagues he had no choice but to face his fears. "Ben would sit behind the driver and consume a case of beer each trip in an attempt to drown away the nightmarish images his memory replayed of that horrible crash," described one reporter.[14] In between sips of Schlitz, he talked endlessly to the bus driver while staring alertly at the road ahead. "Ben searched for signs, and as he did his shoulder jerked left and right and his foot stabbed the floor," described Pat Jordan. "When the bus arrived at its destination, the players would wake to find their manager had consumed all his beer and simply looked more haggard than usual."[15]

Though the trauma of the bus crash contributed to Geraghty's heavy drinking, it paradoxically may have made him a better manager. Jordan hypothesized that the incident caused Geraghty to try and foresee everything before it happened: "He saw beyond his players to the things they'd say and do before they said and did them. And in the process, he began to know his players better than they knew themselves. This deepened perception was what made Ben Geraghty a great manager and a great man, and he owed it to the accident."[16]

Geraghty cared about his players and wanted Aaron, Garner, and Mantilla to feel like they were a part of the team, although circumstances at the time made fitting in difficult. Black players were prohibited from eating in the same restaurants or staying in the same hotels as their teammates. Instead, Geraghty would order burgers and bring them back to the bus. Once the White players were dropped off at the team hotel, the bus would head across town to private homes, the YMCA, or an all-Black hotel to drop off the others. Geraghty always visited the three Black players to talk baseball and race relations over a few beers. On one road trip to Columbus, Georgia, the Braves were invited to a dinner at Fort Benning. The three Black players were forced to eat in the kitchen, where they were joined by Geraghty. "I've known White players and managers who will try to put on a good face around Black players despite their real feelings, but there wasn't a phony bone in Ben's body," recalled Aaron.[17]

Sally League owners feared that Black players would hurt attendance. Instead, the Braves consistently drew capacity crowds wherever they played. Black fans filled their designated sections and cheered boisterously when Aaron, Garner, or Mantilla made the most routine of plays. White fans, some of whom came out just to taunt the dark-skinned players, packed the rest of the ballpark. "When we looked up at all those black and white faces screaming at us, we couldn't help but feel the weight of what we were doing," wrote Aaron.[18]

As the season wore on, Jacksonville's Black players endured hostilities from opposing teams and fans alike. Even some teammates were unhappy about their presence. Just as Robinson had done when he integrated the major leagues, the pioneers of the Sally League had to show restraint in the face of cruel treatment. "The Braves knew, and we knew, that we not only had to play well, but if we ever lost our cool or caused an incident, it might set the whole program back five or ten years," recalled Aaron.[19] At the plate, the Black players were frequently targets of opposing pitchers' fastballs. Mantilla, Garner, and Reedy were first, second, and third in the league at being hit by pitches. Mantilla, who was used to a fiery style of Puerto Rican baseball in which fighting was considered part of the game, was not afraid to retaliate. Geraghty eventually had to ask Aaron to help calm Mantilla down. "You're going to get us killed," said Aaron.[20] Though Mantilla spoke minimal English at the time, he got the message.

For the most part, the Black players had to put their heads down and jog to first base after a beaning or get right back in the batter's box after some chin music. Mantilla recalled one instance, however, when an opposing pitcher's attempt at intimidation backfired. The hurler threw two heaters up and in to Garner, which he managed to avoid. When the third pitch also sailed toward his head, Garner calmly reached up and caught the ball with his bare hand.[21]

The treatment from fans—who hurled threats, racial slurs, and projectiles—was even worse. Years later, Garner would read death threats Aaron received as he neared Babe Ruth's home run record. "Believe me, that hate mail, bad as it is, is no worse than some of the hell we went through that year in the Sally League," said Garner. "I learned some words down there that Webster didn't know."[22]

The only recourse the Black players had was to perform well on the field, and no one in the league hit better than Aaron. The teenage phenom had remarkably quick wrists and raw power that defied his relatively small frame. To that point in his young career, Aaron had been primarily a singles hitter, but Geraghty encouraged him to use more of an uppercut swing to take advantage of his power potential.[23] As a result, Aaron swatted twenty-two home runs—second most in the league—while hitting .362

with 125 RBIs. Though he swung at virtually any pitch from his head to his shoe tops, he almost always made contact, striking out a remarkably low 22 times in 610 plate appearances. Aaron's bat was far more advanced than his second-base defense, however, as evidenced by the thirty-six errors he committed. His glove was, at best, a couple years away from being major league caliber. In the Puerto Rican Winter League, Aaron would transition to the outfield, a switch that propelled his ascension to the big leagues a year later.

Geraghty treated his players with fatherly compassion, but he would give them an earful when they made a mental mistake or missed signs. During games he stood in the corner of the dugout with his hat pulled down so far that it nearly covered his eyes. He groaned and clutched the Saint Christopher medal he wore around his neck when one of his hurlers walked an opposing batter.[24] The players "cringed at his scowl on the playing field because they wanted his approval."[25] No player, Aaron included, was above one of Geraghty's tongue-lashings, though the skipper always did so in private rather than in front of the whole team.

Behind the outstanding play of Aaron, Garner, and Mantilla, plus solid pitching by nineteen-game winners Ray Crone and Larry Lassalle, Geraghty piloted Jacksonville to its first Sally League pennant in twenty-two years. Aaron secured the circuit's Most Valuable Player Award. Geraghty told reporters that by the following year Aaron would make fans forget about Jackie Robinson.[26] "I knew that was nonsense," said Aaron of the compliment, "but Ben's faith meant a lot to me."[27]

Fans certainly never forgot Robinson, but Aaron put his own stamp on the game—to say the least. Two seasons later, he made the National League All-Star team and reached the twenty-home run plateau, a mark he would achieve every year for two decades. His consistent power over such an extended period catapulted him past Babe Ruth for the all-time home run record. Aaron played for more than a dozen managers in his career and said that none compared to Ben Geraghty. "He was the greatest manager I ever played for, perhaps the greatest manager who ever lived, and that includes managers in the big leagues," declared Aaron. "I've never played for a guy who could get more out of every ballplayer than he could. He knew how to communicate with everybody and to treat every player as an individual."[28]

CHAPTER 11

During Geraghty's first two years in Jacksonville, sportswriters around the Sally League had slowly gotten to know the aloof skipper and took to calling him the "Great Stone Face" because of his lack of expression. Geraghty, who startled easily and always seemed on edge, was described at various times as grim, pessimistic, quiet, and restless. After wins and away from the ballpark, however, he could be garrulous with players and journalists, as long as the discussion revolved around his favorite topic. "Change the subject from baseball, and you've lost a conversation partner," summed up one reporter.[29] In this way, Geraghty was similar to his mentor, Casey Stengel, who would regularly regale sportswriters with stories at the hotel bar until closing time. Neither man had many interests outside of baseball; they were completely dedicated to the sport.

"[Geraghty's] endless chatter will sometimes have you getting home at 3 a.m. but happy you stayed late to hear what he had to say," wrote one Sally League scribe.[30] He would opine for hours about the art of bunting and other baseball strategies and carried on about how the difference between winning and losing is pitching. If the topic of the Spokane Indians' bus crash came up, however, he was less loquacious. "It was bad," Geraghty said softly to one reporter without adding further commentary.[31] Sometimes he would mention that George Lyden had asked him to switch seats on the bus. "An hour later we went over an embankment, and the kid who took my seat was killed instantly," he told another reporter.[32]

Even without Hammerin' Hank's booming bat, Geraghty led Jacksonville to another Sally League pennant in 1954 behind the league's best defense and outstanding pitching by Humberto Robinson and Bob Trowbridge. That winter, Geraghty took an offseason job managing in the Puerto Rican Winter League. Like other players and managers in the relatively low-paying minor-league sector, he always found employment in between baseball seasons. The previous winter, he had worked for an appliance business but talked more about baseball than the televisions he was trying to sell.[33] Managing in winter ball was certainly a better utilization of his skill set. In Puerto Rico, Geraghty piloted the Criollos de Caguas, a team that featured several players from the Braves organization. Caguas ultimately advanced to the league championship against the Cangrejeros de Santurce, whose roster included Willie Mays and nineteen-year-old Dodgers farmhand Roberto Clemente. Santurce took down Caguas in five games. "I've been in baseball for nearly 20 years, and outside a cup of coffee with the Dodgers and a ham sandwich with the Braves, all my time has been in the minors. But I still have to say that Mays is the best ballplayer I've ever seen," Geraghty declared.[34] Had Caguas defeated Santurce, Geraghty's team would have advanced to the Caribbean Series and played a Venezuelan team anchored by Jack Lohrke.

Geraghty's reputation as a tactician, motivator, and—perhaps most importantly—a winner had become widely recognized in baseball circles. As a result, he received managerial offers from several higher-ranking minor league teams in other organizations. Geraghty turned down the overtures to remain in the Braves' system, hoping that his dedication would result in a promotion to the parent club. With only sixteen major league teams at the time, becoming a major league manager was a tough fraternity to break into. "You've gotta wait for that one opportunity," Geraghty told reporters.[35]

Geraghty piloted the Jacksonville Braves to second and first place finishes over the next two summers. In the latter season, he became only the second manager to win three Sally League pennants and won the league's Manager of the Year Award. Ironically, he marked the ten-year anniversary of the Spokane Indians tragedy with a tense bus ride through Tennessee's Smoky Mountains on a road trip to Knoxville. During the winter of 1955–1956, Geraghty led Caguas to the Caribbean Series while taking home the league's top manager award for the second winter in a row.[36]

By then, Geraghty had established a clear pattern of success regardless of where he managed or the players on his roster. In Jacksonville, Geraghty got the most out of farmhands like Wes Covington, Mike Roarke, Joe Morgan, and Juan Pizarro. Roarke and Morgan soaked up knowledge from their manager as Geraghty had done with Stengel. "Mike Roarke and I would have a few beers with Ben after games and go over all aspects of the game," recalled Morgan six decades later. "Three true Irishmen!"[37]

Geraghty's track record in Bristol, Jacksonville, and Puerto Rico put him in line for a promotion. "Those who have followed Ben Geraghty closely believe he's ripe for a shot at the major leagues," wrote sportswriter Gene Thompson.[38] Geraghty would have to wait longer for his shot at a big league job, but he got closer than ever when the Milwaukee brass elevated him to the manager's seat of the Triple A Wichita Braves in 1957. Wichita had finished the prior season in seventh place with a 65–88 record and returned six pitchers, three infielders, and two outfielders. Geraghty would once again be put to the test. In Milwaukee, meanwhile, manager Fred Haney faced pressure to win the pennant following four consecutive second- or third-place finishes.

Only one step from the majors, Geraghty could now use his abilities as a brilliant baseball strategist, talent evaluator, and psychologist to directly impact the parent club. In his years of experience, he developed a belief that winning had more to do with mindset and hustle than physical ability.[39] Hustle, in his mind, was contagious and could spread from one player to another. "Your head is as useful as your arms, legs, and eyes," he would say. That was, after all, how Geraghty stuck around as a player as long as he did. "A lot of guys could hit and field better, so there must have been a reason they didn't shove me down lower than [Class-A ball]. I think the reason was hustle and study."[40] He focused on the means of success, not the ends.

Geraghty mastered the art of learning what motivated each player. He turned anything that could be perceived as a slight into something malicious. A newspaper's hint of criticism about his team's play could be twisted into an insult on the family name that warranted payback on the field. On one occasion, his team's batting practice was cut short by a few minutes to accommodate a pregame ceremony. Geraghty convinced his team that they were being deprived and rallied his troops to rout the opponent.[41] Geraghty knew his players "inside-out, what made them tick, the quirks of their individual personalities, how they thought, responded, and felt," wrote Jordan. "He knew how to improve their baseball talents and, more important, how to make them better men."[42]

In Wichita, Geraghty impacted the big league Braves in tangible ways. Early on, he helped a struggling Wes Covington get back on track after the outfielder's demotion from Milwaukee. Covington hit twenty-one home runs after his promotion back to the majors. Later in the season, Milwaukee needed an outfielder to replace the injured Bill Bruton and asked Wichita for power hitter Ray Shearer. Geraghty instead recommended Bob Hazle, who had been previously released by the Cincinnati Reds and was coming off a serious knee injury the year before. Hazle was a streaky hitter whose numbers were not as robust as Shearer's, but Geraghty liked the way Hazle was swinging the bat. "He's the one who can help you because he's just getting hot," Geraghty told the Milwaukee executives.[43] Hazle proceeded to hit like peak Ted Williams, batting .403 with seven home runs in forty-one games with Milwaukee. He was as important as any player on the team down the stretch. Milwaukee's ninety-five wins earned them the National League pennant and seemingly saved Haney's job. In the World Series, the Braves took down Casey Stengel's mighty Yankees in seven games. Besides Hazle, many of Geraghty's former pupils—Aaron, Covington, Mantilla, Crone, and Pizzaro—played key roles for the champs.

While Geraghty made contributions that buoyed Milwaukee, he also steered Wichita to a highly successful season. As he had done at his previous posts, Geraghty instilled a winning attitude and quickly turned Wichita's fortunes. Despite a spate of injuries and players shuttling to and from Milwaukee, Geraghty's squad exceeded expectations, improving by twenty-eight wins while topping the second-place Denver Bears by three games to win the American Association title. Wichita's success resulted in more awards for Geraghty's mantel. He was the unanimous choice for the American Association Manager of the Year Award and was voted by *The Sporting News* as the top skipper in all of minor league baseball. Geraghty's face graced the front page of America's preeminent sports publication on January 1, 1958. "Geraghty's work in 1957 confirmed what the Braves already knew—that he knows how to manage," wrote Bob Burnes. "In 11 seasons, his clubs have finished out of the first division only twice. Four have been pennant winners."[44]

Geraghty's successful first season at Wichita earned him a sizeable raise in 1958. Before the season he laid out four goals he wanted to achieve in his career: winning the Junior World Series (the Triple A title between winners of the American Association and International League), winning a major league pennant, winning the World Series, and making the National Baseball Hall of Fame as a manager. "I've got my heart set on it, and I'll do it someday," he said in a rare show of optimism.[45] Geraghty's lofty goals were not far-fetched, given that he was only forty-six years old and had accumulated an impressive list of accomplishments.

Milwaukee pilfered Wichita of several players in 1958, including Carlton Willey, Casey Wise, Mel Roach, and Joe Koppe. Still, Wichita finished in second place. Geraghty "makes much of skimpy material and wins hands down with equal talent. Somehow, he transfers his go-at-top-speed-every-minute personal credo to every player he manages," opined Robert Phipps of the *Evening World-Herald*.[46] Geraghty was honored by the city and team with "Ben Geraghty Night" in the final home game of the season. Fans pooled a substantial monetary gift, and his team paid homage by smashing five home runs.

By then, Ben and Mary had five children: Patrick, Mary Elizabeth, Barry, Thomas, and Benjamin Jr. That fall, Patrick enrolled at Marquette University, where he played football, and the Geraghtys moved to the Milwaukee area. The relocation was possibly made with the expectation that Geraghty would eventually be elevated to the parent club. An offer to manage the Braves was not yet forthcoming, however, and Geraghty signed on to again manage the Triple A affiliate, which transferred from Wichita to Louisville and adopted the name Colonels.

Louisville sportswriters were not sure what to make of their dour new manager. One scribe from the *Courier-Journal* described that someone encountering Geraghty for the first time might be inclined to ask, "When did the late departed go and how are the survivors taking it?"[47] Particularly after a tough loss or during a losing streak, the introverted Geraghty could become "positively antisocial."[48] There was one exception, however. Ben called Mary following road games—win or lose.[49]

Louisville's shortstop in 1959 was Ted Kazanski, a Michigander with six years of big league experience under his belt. Looking back several decades later, he had fond memories of his one season playing for Geraghty. "I thought he was great with the pitchers and knowing how to run a pitching staff," recalled Kazanski. "We got along good together. Off the field, he was a good man and a real gentleman. He took a shine to me for some reason. He really liked his beer. One night, after a game, I was in bed and the phone rang. When you get a call at two in the morning, it's never good news. I picked it up reluctantly, and it was Ben. He said, 'What are you doin'? I said, 'Ben, What the hell do you think I'm doin'? It's two in the morning, I'm sleeping!' He said, 'how 'bout comin' down to my room for a while?' I went over to his room, and he had a whole bathtub full of ice and beer. We sat there drinking beer until the morning talking baseball. He loved the game."[50]

Louisville traveled by airplane, which to Geraghty was no less stressful than riding a bus. Louisville player John DeMerit distinctly recalled

Geraghty having a death grip on the seat handles during flights.[51] An incident during the 1959 season did little to quell his fears. The Colonels' plane made an emergency landing in Denver after an engine went out. "They had the crash truck out and fire wagon out," described Geraghty. "I thought, 'This is it.' I always did like train travel better."[52]

Travel scares aside, Geraghty's first season in Louisville was a rousing success and his winningest as a manager. The Colonels racked up ninety-seven wins and Geraghty captured his fifth minor league pennant. Yet when the Braves' managerial post opened with Fred Haney's resignation on October 4, owner Lou Perini summarily ruled out Geraghty, citing his lack of name recognition and big league experience. "I would think that [Leo] Durocher would possibly fit the description of the type of manager we will be looking for," said one club official.[53] Milwaukee ultimately settled on Chuck Dressen, who had managed parts of ten big league seasons and won a pair of pennants with the Dodgers. Geraghty publicly supported the organization's decision: "I think Dressen coming into our organization will mean a big difference to our personnel in Milwaukee. The boys will be better off."[54] Geraghty turned down the Phillies' third-base coaching job, as he had done with previous big league coaching offers. His preference was to manage in the minors, which he believed was a better stepping-off point to his goal of managing in the big leagues. To that end, he signed on for another year in Louisville and patiently awaited his chance.

Geraghty's plight was not lost on baseball observers. "As long as owners keep screening managers as if they were casting a TV spectacular, men like Geraghty need not apply," wrote Jack Mann in *Newsday*. "He's just a good baseball man, that's all."[55]

The 1960 Colonels roster included nine players who had never played Triple A ball before, including DeMerit and Howie Bedell, both of whom held fond memories of Geraghty more than sixty years later.

"I thought [Geraghty] was excellent at evaluating personnel," recalled DeMerit, a Wisconsin native. "He was a little on the gruff side. If he didn't like what was going on, you heard it from him. He was kind enough to take you aside rather than lay it on you in public. I thought he was spot on in his analysis. From that standpoint, he was an excellent manager."[56]

Geraghty's run at another American Association pennant was derailed when he was hospitalized on May 5 with stomach ulcers. Braves chief scout

Bill Adair filled in as interim manager. Geraghty was prescribed medication and ordered to rest for six months, which meant his season was over. In his absence, the Colonels finished in third place but won the league playoffs and defeated the Toronto Maple Leafs in the Junior World Series.

"I've found ulcers and baseball just don't mix," said Geraghty while recovering at his Milwaukee home. "Between the good play of the team and some big pills the doc gave me, I'm relaxed for the first time in years. I've even quit biting my nails, and that's a habit I've had ever since I've been in baseball."[57] He failed to mention whether he intended to quit drinking, a habit with more devastating consequences, which—along with the high level of anxiety associated with his occupation—undoubtedly contributed to his gastric ailment.

Geraghty perhaps sensed that time was running out on fulfilling his dream. After his prolonged absence, he was more vocal about his desire to manage in the big leagues. "I feel better and younger than I have in years," he told one reporter. "I'll be back in action next season. I feel like I'm closer than ever to my goal of being a major-league manager."[58]

That fall, the Geraghty family moved to West Palm Beach, Florida, and Ben returned to work as skipper for the Braves' Florida Winter Instructional League team in Bradenton. The sixty-game circuit, which ran from September to November, featured top prospects from six big league teams. The Braves' entry included Joe Torre, Phil Niekro, Tommie Aaron (Henry's younger brother), and a bonus baby hurler named Pat Jordan.

Jordan's 1974 memoir *A False Spring* reflected on his three-year minor-league career, including his stint playing for Geraghty in winter ball. Jordan vividly described meeting Geraghty for the first time: "He was sitting—naked but for a towel wrapped around his waist—on a low stool in front of a locker. His legs were crossed, and he was sucking from a can of beer, which he then drained in a long gulp, his head tilted far back, and tossed into a large aluminum pail before reaching down to rip another can from the six-pack beside his stool." Jordan remembered shaking Geraghty's frail hand and looking into his piercing eyes. "They were unbelievably blue and penetrating," wrote Jordan, "and yet they seemed distracted too, and terror-stricken, so you could not look at them for very long without the feeling that they were looking through and beyond you at some distant vision."[59]

By then, Geraghty was forty-eight, but his body—battered in the bus crash and abused by years of heavy drinking—had aged beyond his years. He was rail thin and wore bags under his eyes. His face and neck bore a reddish hue from sun exposure, but the rest of his body had a grayish tone. Geraghty's failing health prohibited him from throwing batting practice or hitting fungoes. Even walking from the dugout to the mound for a pitching change had become a chore. Mostly, he directed his coaches and players from his perch in the corner of the dugout. Though Geraghty had wilted physically, his mind remained razor sharp. "He absorbed every shade and nuance of the game until there was no situation to which he, as a manager, could not adjust," recalled Jordan. "This consumed his waking life. Sitting on the team bus or in a hotel room or bar or dugout, he proposed—out loud—a hundred hypothetical situations that he resolved in a dozen different ways before finding the most satisfactory solution. At times his players thought him mad."[60]

Geraghty recovered from his ulcers and returned to Louisville's dugout in 1961. Joe Torre began the season as the Colonels' catcher, but his outstanding hitting earned him a call-up to Milwaukee in May. Bob Uecker, who had broken camp with the Braves, was sent down to Louisville. One of baseball's great comedians, Uecker brought a levity to the clubhouse that proved to be a good balance to Geraghty's workmanlike approach. "If there was some screwy activity going on, Ben knew where to point his finger," recalled Howie Bedell. "But as serious as Ben was, I got the feeling that he sensed just how special a guy Uecker was. Bob kept things alive."[61]

Bedell, a native of Pottstown, Pennsylvania, was the Colonels' leadoff man that season and one of the fastest players to ever play the game. The 1961 season did not start well for the fleet-footed outfielder, however. He was not squaring up many balls, and even when he did make solid contact the hits weren't falling. In the midst of his struggles, Geraghty asked him to come to the ballpark for an early workout. When Bedell arrived at 9:00 a.m. the next day, he was surprised to find the only people there were the trainer, coaches Ken Silvestri and George Susce, and Geraghty. Bedell took batting practice for ninety minutes under Geraghty's watchful eye. The skipper then asked the twenty-five-year-old to sit next to him in the dugout. Bedell expected to hear he was being demoted. Instead, Geraghty told him to forget about the last two weeks and assured him that he was going to be his leadoff man and have a heck of a year. Geraghty repeated himself several times, as if he was willing it to happen. He said it in a way that reminded Bedell of his father. That night, Bedell started a forty-three-game hitting streak and wound up hitting .327 for the season. He played in the major leagues with the Braves a year later and considered Geraghty's encouraging words the turning point in his career.[62]

As Bedell struck up a friendship with Geraghty, the two had conversations about the Spokane Indians' bus crash. "He would get very emotional about it," recalled Bedell. "I think his heavy drinking came about as a result of the accident; it's what changed his whole life."[63]

While Geraghty's Colonels got off to another terrific start, the Milwaukee Braves struggled under Dressen, who was fired in September and replaced by Birdie Tebbetts. Geraghty was overlooked once again. He believed the Braves had not given him a chance in the majors because he was "doing a good job developing their young players."[64] There may had been some truth to that. He was such a stickler for fundamentals that his players were ready for The Show when given the opportunity. "When a player got through Geraghty and into the big leagues," recalled Chuck Cottier, "the major-league manager didn't have to worry about, Can this guy bunt? Can he hit-and-run? Does he know when to steal a base? Can a pitcher field his position? With Geraghty, it made no difference who you were or what you had done previously. If you didn't execute all of the fundamentals, you didn't play for him."[65]

Ted Kazanski offered another possible explanation as to why Geraghty was bypassed: "I thought he never got his due as a manager, and I think that was because of his demeanor, his personality. He was just too quiet, and if you're a big league manager you've got to bullshit those guys, and I don't think Ben could do that. He was so quiet, and I couldn't picture him handling the media."[66]

Though Geraghty was certainly an asset in the minor leagues and was not the most adept at handling the press, his reputation as an alcoholic undoubtedly factored in keeping him out of a big league managerial seat. Bedell went on to a career as a baseball executive and later asked other front office personnel why Geraghty never got his chance. He learned that the Braves respected his ability to manage a ball game and his handling of players, but they were never going to let him manage the big league club because of his drinking.[67]

Passed over by the Braves for a third time, Geraghty now realized that his dream of managing in Milwaukee would never be fulfilled. After a second-place finish and Junior World Series loss to the Buffalo Bisons in 1961, he left Louisville and the Braves organization and took a job with the newly relocated Jacksonville Suns of the International League. The majority owner of the Jacksonville franchise was Bobby Maduro, a Cuban entrepreneur whose club had originally played in Havana as the Sugar Kings before political unrest forced the team's relocation to Jersey City in 1960. Geraghty's three-year contract made him the highest paid manager in the minor leagues.

That offseason Geraghty dealt with more health tribulations. On January 29, 1962, he underwent a four-hour operation for a circulatory problem. Some media outlets described it as a cardiac procedure while other reports indicated the ailment involved an artery to the stomach. Despite the seriousness of the procedure, he was in Jacksonville's dugout when the season began.

Geraghty returned to familiar environs but his team—an affiliate of the Cleveland Indians—was new to him. One of his first decisions was to convert Vic Davalillo—a pitcher in his first four professional seasons—to a full-time outfielder. The move proved to be another shrewd decision by Geraghty. Davalillo, a Venezuelan, hit .346 to lead the International League and went on to have a sixteen-year major league career. The Suns finished with a 94–60 record and captured the league title—Geraghty's sixth—before losing to the Atlanta Crackers in the league playoffs. Geraghty was again named his league's manager of the year. He was rumored to be a managerial candidate for the Washington Senators' and Cleveland Indians' vacancies, but neither job materialized.

Tommy John, still just a teenager, pitched for the Suns down the stretch in 1962 and at the beginning of the 1963 season. He later described his impression of Geraghty in his memoir: "[He] was a soft-spoken Irishman with a face so deeply graven you could have planted corn in his wrinkles. To me, at 19, he looked as old as my grandfather . . . he just looked bent and discouraged and worn down."[68]

"Sometimes after a game, he would sit there silently for an hour in his baggy long johns and sweatshirt, smoking, smoking, smoking, gulping a swallow now and then from a can of beer, and seeming to play all over again in his mind a game we had lost."[69]

John, who would become best known for the novel elbow surgery that extended his career and bears his name, eventually won 288 games during his twenty-six seasons in the big leagues. He did not see much action on Geraghty's watch, however. Though John made the team out of spring training, Geraghty didn't use him because he didn't throw hard.[70] John surmised that the fact he did not drink alcohol may have been another strike against him. "Ben was from the old school," recalled John. "He liked guys who would go out and drink after the game, and I didn't drink. I was like an outsider to him."[71] John was thrilled when he was demoted to Double A Charleston, where he could pitch for Johnny Lipon, a manager who had confidence in him.

Besides John, Jacksonville's pitching staff in 1963 also included Sonny Siebert and Mike Cuellar, who would go on to win a combined 325 games in the majors, and Ruben Gomez, who already had 76 big league wins under his belt. Despite the talented roster, the Suns performed miserably to start the season. "We were supposed to have a pretty good year, but everything went south, and we were just terrible," recalled Gordy Lund. "We had a veteran ballclub, and for whatever reason a bunch of us had bad years, and I think that took a toll on [Geraghty]."[72]

A doubleheader sweep at the hands of the Atlanta Crackers on Sunday, June 16, dropped Jacksonville to thirteen games below .500—nearly unheard of for a Geraghty-managed team. It had been a stressful two months for a man who loathed losing more than anything. Jacksonville team president Sam Wolfson had warned Geraghty that he was going to worry himself to death.[73] The emotional stress and years of smoking and drinking proved to be too much. In the early morning hours of June 18, Ben complained to Mary of throat and chest pain. Within hours, he was dead of an apparent heart attack at age fifty.[74]

During Geraghty's seventeen-year minor league managing career, he compiled 1,317 wins and 1,021 losses for a winning percentage of .563, a mark higher than the major league winning percentages of Walter Alston, Bobby

Cox, Miller Huggins, Sparky Anderson, Leo Durocher, Casey Stengel, Tony LaRussa, and countless other Hall of Fame skippers. Whether Geraghty's success would have translated into similar success in the big leagues will never be known. "His record was amazing. He was a completely dedicated man," said Stengel of his protégé.[75]

Geraghty received numerous posthumous honors, including inductions in the Florida Sports and St. Benedict Preparatory halls of fame. Jacksonville established an award for meritorious service in baseball in his name. Aaron was bestowed the honor in 1970. In his acceptance speech, Aaron said that his biggest disappointment in baseball was that Geraghty did not get promoted to the major leagues when he did.[76]

Geraghty's legacy lived on through his players who went on to have scouting, coaching, and managerial careers of their own. Mike Roarke enjoyed several decades as a minor league manager and big league pitching coach after his playing career. Another of Ben's pupils, Joe Morgan, managed the Boston Red Sox from 1988 to 1991. "I learned a lot of baseball from Ben Geraghty," recalled Morgan. "He taught me to never let a pitcher throw one more pitch when he was cooked. Get him out of there even if he is your best pitcher. Ben should have managed in the big leagues and should have gotten there before I did."[77]

Geraghty was a mentor to many and knew the game like no one else. In the words of Bedell, "He was the ultimate baseball man."[78]

12

LUCKY

After packing on weight during the winter, Jack Lohrke went to spring training in 1948 looking to build on his solid rookie campaign. He got off to an auspicious start, leading the powerful Giants with eight home runs during the exhibition schedule.[1] The sophomore big leaguer maintained a hot bat when the regular season began, blasting round-trippers in two of the Giants' first three contests. New York's entire lineup soon slumped, however, posting a collective .200 batting average from May 9 to May 21.[2] Manager Mel Ott, looking to reignite the offense, benched Lohrke in favor of Sid Gordon.

At the All-Star break, the fourth-place Giants were a game below .500, a disappointing eight games back of the upstart Boston Braves. The defending National League champion Dodgers, a half-game behind their crosstown rivals, were also underachieving. Leo Durocher had returned to Brooklyn's dugout following a year-long suspension, but his relationship with Branch Rickey and owner Larry MacPhail had soured. On July 16, the season took a stunning turn when Ott resigned his managerial post and was replaced by Durocher. Giants' owner Horace Stoneham and Ott had discussed a change in preceding days, and both agreed the Giants should try to land Durocher. Stoneham received permission from league president Ford Frick to approach the Dodgers about hiring Durocher. Once Rickey granted Stoneham permission, the dominoes fell rapidly. Burt Shotton, who had piloted the Dodgers to within one game of a World Series title a year earlier as interim manager, replaced Durocher in Brooklyn.

The reaction among Giants fans was as divisive as Durocher himself. "From today on, I am an ex-Giant fan," exclaimed one woman on Fifth Avenue. Her companion chimed in: "We couldn't beat the Dodgers under Mel Ott, so we had to get a manager who can. Durocher may be the guy. Personally, I don't like him, but you can't win pennants with love."[3]

Another Giants rooter was ecstatic: "Durocher is the best manager in baseball. With that Giant power, he'll blow the league apart."[4]

On Durocher's first day at the helm, he said he intended to play Lohkre regularly. "I have always considered Jack Lohrke a real good prospect," Durocher told the *New York Times*.[5] But Lohrke's path to more playing time was summarily derailed by a severe case of tonsillitis, which landed him in Cincinnati's Christ Hospital on July 19.[6] He rejoined the team a few days later in St. Louis and then underwent a tonsillectomy upon his return to the Big Apple.

Twenty-five months to the day after the Spokane Indians' bus crash, a similar tragedy struck the Duluth Dukes, a St. Louis Cardinals' farm team in the Class C Northern League. A bus carrying seventeen members of the team was traveling from Eau Claire, Wisconsin, to St. Cloud, Minnesota, moving westbound on Highway 36 just north of St. Paul when a truck carrying dry ice crossed the median and struck the bus head-on. The bus careened into a ditch and burst into flames, killing four players and the driver of the truck. A fifth player died two days later. Among the survivors were future big league manager Mel McGaha and Elmer Schoendienst, whose brother Red had a Hall of Fame career.

Reminiscent of the Spokane Indians' 1946 incident, minor league benefit games were staged across the country in the weeks that followed, raising $64,090 for the victims and their families.[7] The Dukes received more support in the form of replacements than the Indians had as an independent franchise. The Cardinals and seven other Northern League rivals all loaned players to help Duluth field a team and complete the season. The results were similar to the Indians' post-crash team of 1946; Duluth had been six games above .500 before the crash and went 13–27 after.

Lohrke remained sidelined while recuperating from his tonsillectomy until August 10. By then, the Giants were playing winning baseball and Gordon was hitting over .300 as Durocher's regular third sacker. Lohrke remained in a reserve role until September, when he took over the starting second-base job and leadoff spot in the batting order. He finished the season strong, compiling nine multi-hit games in September to raise his average from the low .200s to .250.

Mentions of Lohrke in newspapers at the time usually included his nickname. When he went four for four with a homer against Pittsburgh on September 2, the *New York Times* wrote, "The authority in a brace of home runs exploded by Walk Cooper and Lucky Jack Lohrke swept Larry Jansen to his sixteenth victory of the campaign on Forbes Field today as the Giants conquered the Pirates, 5 to 4."[8] It was a catchy moniker that stuck.

Though he enjoyed success at baseball's highest level, the highlight of Jack's year occurred away from the baseball diamond. On December 10, 1948, he and Marie tied the knot in Los Angeles. News of their nuptials ran in papers across the country, many of which referenced Jack's string of good fortune.

Lohrke's name came up in offseason trade speculation before the 1949 season. One rumor had him going to the Chicago Cubs.[9] Another had him off to Pittsburgh for pitcher Kirby Higbe.[10] When the season began, Lohrke was still a Giant, but he had a new look, donning glasses for the first time. He shuffled between second and third base for the first month of the season before he was sent down to Jersey City for ten days in May because infielder Dick Culler needed two more weeks of service time to qualify for the major league pension program.[11] Lohrke was recalled as soon as Culler met the minimum tenure, then enjoyed one of the best games of his career on May 31 against the Dodgers at the Polo Grounds. Hitting leadoff and playing shortstop, Lohrke tattooed a home run and laced three doubles in six at-bats. His performance overshadowed a productive day by Jackie Robinson, who singled three times in five trips for Brooklyn. The Dodgers prevailed in fourteen innings.

Despite carrying a solid .259 batting average, Lohrke was sent back to Jersey City on July 5 to make room for Hank Thompson, a fellow Battle of the Bulge veteran who joined Monte Irvin as the first Black players to suit up for the Giants. Thompson, twenty-three, was hitting .296 with fourteen home runs in Triple A at the time of his call-up. Lohrke maintained a positive attitude in spite of the demotion. "I want to play regularly and know that with the Jerseys, I will get that opportunity," Lohrke told the *Bayonne Times*. "Sitting on the bench was not helping me and I'm glad that Durocher is willing to give me a chance to become a great player."[12] There were rumors in the media that a touch of jealousy may have contributed to Lohrke being jettisoned to the minors. Durocher's leading lady wife, Laraine Day, had reportedly batted her eyes at the good-looking infielder.[13] Lohrke remained in Jersey City through the end of the minor league season, hitting .302 with ten homers in eighty-one games. He was recalled to New York down the stretch and appeared in seven games for the fifth-place Giants.

Lohrke added to his unique list of life experiences in 1949 with an appearance on the big screen. He made a cameo in *The Monte Stratton Story*, a film based on the Chicago White Sox pitcher who required a leg amputation related to a hunting accident. Jimmy Stewart played the part of Stratton. His costar, June Allyson, asked Lohrke for his autograph during filming.[14]

Durocher noticed that Lohrke possessed sinking movement on his throws to first base and worked him out as a pitcher in the spring of 1950. Two other third basemen—Bob Lemon and Bucky Walters—had made similar conversions to the mound with good success. Durocher observed that Lohrke threw harder than Walters when he made the switch. The experiment was abandoned when the season began, though Lohrke eventually took the mound with some regularity later in his career. During the 1950 season, he was relegated to a utility role and started only six games, even though he was on the Giants' roster for the entire season. Serving almost exclusively as a pinch hitter and defensive replacement, he recorded eight hits in forty-three at-bats for an average of .186.

With Eddie Stanky at second base, Al Dark at shortstop, and the combination of Hank Thompson and Bobby Thomson manning third, Lohrke again received few opportunities in 1951. In one of his rare starts, an April 23 game against the Phillies at Shibe Park, he went two for three and hit his only home run of the season. Philadelphia's center fielder that day was Richie Ashburn, who had been Vic Picetti's teammate at the All-American game in 1944. Ashburn, one of the best young players in the game and an eventual Hall of Famer, went three for four with a pair of RBIs for the victorious Phillies.

A twenty-year-old outfielder named Willie Mays debuted for the Giants on May 25, 1951. "The Say Hey Kid" managed only one hit in his first twenty-six at-bats, but Durocher stuck with him. Mays rebounded to hit .288 with nineteen home runs the rest of the way while playing magnificent center-field defense. At the All-Star break, the Giants held a 44–36 record but trailed the juggernaut Dodgers by eight games. By August 11, Brooklyn had extended its stronghold to a seemingly insurmountable thirteen games. The Giants then proceeded to reel off sixteen consecutive victories in late August, cutting the deficit to five games. In September, Durocher's crew won twenty of twenty-five to track down their rivals from Flatbush. When the season ended on September 30, the Giants and Dodgers were dead even. The pennant would be decided by a best-of-three playoff.

The Dodgers and Giants split the first two games, setting up a decisive third game at the Polo Grounds on October 3. A pair of twenty-game winners—the Dodgers' Don Newcombe and the Giants' Sal Maglie—locked horns in a duel that lived up to the billing. The game was tied at one after seven innings, but Brooklyn pushed three runs across in the eighth off Maglie to take a 4–1 lead. Down to their last three outs in the bottom of the ninth, the first two Giants—Dark and Don Mueller—reached on consecutive singles. After Irvin fouled out to first base, Whitey Lockman doubled to left field, scoring Dark and sending Mueller to third. When Mueller slid into the bag, he injured his ankle and had to be carried off the field. Clint Hartung pinch-ran and Lohrke was told to get loose; he would play third base if the game went to extra innings.

With the Scotland-born, Staten Island–raised Thomson coming to the plate, Brooklyn manager Chuck Dressen replaced Newcombe with Ralph Branca, who had thrown 135 pitches only two days earlier. Branca's second pitch was high and inside, but Thomson turned on it and sent "the shot heard 'round the world" into the left-field stands, giving the Giants a 5–4 victory. Lohrke and his teammates mobbed Thomson as he crossed home plate.

Having captured the National League crown, the Giants faced the formidable Yankees in the World Series. The Bronx Bombers were piloted by Casey Stengel, who had landed the job after three winning seasons with the Oakland Oaks. With Stengel at the helm, the Yankees had won the previous two Fall Classics. Joe DiMaggio was in the twilight of his career, but rookie Mickey Mantle had emerged as a star, and Yogi Berra was in MVP form. The Giants and Yankees split the first two games at Yankee Stadium but Mantle stepped on a drainpipe while chasing after a fly ball in Game 2 and suffered torn knee ligaments. Despite losing their young stud, Stengel's squad won three of the next four to capture the crown. Lohrke made pinch-hitting appearances in Games 4 and 5 and was hitless in both of his at-bats.

That offseason, the Giants traded Lohrke to Philadelphia for minor-league pitcher Jake Schmitt. The Phillies, two years removed from a pennant-winning season, were led by Ashburn and ace pitcher Robin Roberts. The change of scenery failed to produce more playing time for Lohrke, who appeared in only twenty-five games during the 1952 season. After riding the bench for the first two months of the 1953 campaign, Lohrke was sent to the Triple A Baltimore Orioles, where he spent the rest of the summer. He was replaced on the Phillies roster by nineteen-year-old infielder Ted Kazanski, who, seventy years later, would vividly recall asking teammates why everyone called Jack "Lucky."[15]

In 1954, the Phillies sent Lohrke, right-handed reliever Andy Hansen, and $70,000 to the Pirates in exchange for pitcher and Lohrke's former Santa Fe Division comrade Murry Dickson. The Pirates subsequently assigned Lohrke to the Hollywood Stars in the Pacific Coast League. He played every day for the first time in years and performed well, hitting .263 with eight homers and doing so near his hometown. Lohrke spent two seasons with the Stars before heading north to toil with the Seattle Rainiers and then the Portland Beavers.

In his three seasons in the Pacific Northwest, the bespectacled Lohrke was literally a jack-of-all-trades. He played all four infield spots, caught a number of games, and served as a relief pitcher. In 1957, he made a career-high fourteen appearances on the mound for the Rainiers and even won a game. Injuries began to crop up, however. Lohrke suffered a badly fractured finger from a foul tip while catching and then dislocated a shoulder, maladies that kept him on the sidelines for several weeks at a time. In 1959, Lohrke's final year in pro ball, the thirty-five-year-old had a stint as player-manager in Kennewick, Washington, only 150 miles from Spokane. He was let go for economic reasons on June 29.[16] Lohrke took a coaching job with the Sacramento Solons the following year. Midway through the season, the team was drawing poorly and had to make financial cuts. The axe again fell on Lohrke.

Jack then turned to work outside of baseball, finding employment in the security industry, first with Aerojet—a rocket and missile propulsion manufacturer—and then the Lawrence Livermore Laboratory, a research institution involved in national security, including nuclear weapon design. In 1971, he took a job with the Lockheed Corporation and moved his family to San Jose. Given his stoic and quiet personality, Lohrke was well suited for high-level security work. In one instance, he was tasked with leaving an unmarked bag in a locker at Los Angeles International Airport. Jack did not know its contents, nor did he ask questions. Among his other assignments was providing security for the *Glomar Explorer*, a six-hundred-foot ship with a giant claw that the CIA used to covertly retrieve part of a sunken Russian nuclear submarine from the Pacific Ocean floor. Lohrke retired from Lockheed in 1986 and kept busy with fishing, masonry, and woodwork.

Jack and Marie raised two sons, Kurt and John, and four daughters, Karen, Kathryn, Kim, and Kristina. While Jack supported the family financially through baseball and security work, Marie took care of the kids and maintained a tidy home. Both sons eventually became involved in baseball; Kurt played three seasons in the Boston Red Sox organization, and John has enjoyed a long tenure as general manager of the semipro Alaska Goldpanners, host of the famed Midnight Sun Game every summer solstice. Karen went to college and settled in Spokane, where she works as curator of education at the Jundt Art Museum on the campus of Gonzaga University. Two of her father's baseball cards are proudly displayed on the wall of her office.

Jack remained connected to baseball through friendships with several fellow ex-Giants, including Larry Jansen, Whitey Lockman, Bobby Thomson, and Wes Westrum. Lohrke participated in multiple Old-Timers' games over the years, including a Spokane Indians' reunion game in 1986. Joe Faria was the only other player from the 1946 team to attend. On occasion, Lohrke took his kids to the San Francisco Giants clubhouse at Candlestick Park for visits in the Giants' clubhouse with former teammates Jansen and Mays. Later in life, Lohrke regularly watched Giants' games on television and sometimes became animated if an infielder made a spectacular play or a batter took a ball to the hand or wrist. It was as if he could feel the batter's pain by memory.

Lohrke once attended a birthday party for Rudy Mello, who was an excellent amateur player at Oakland's McClymonds High School in the 1940s. Lohrke and Mello sat in the corner and enjoyed reminiscing about their playing days. Mello recalled the awesome talent of another Bay Area ballplayer—Vic Picetti. Mello shook his head at the thought of Picetti's tragic ending and unfulfilled potential.

For the most part, however, Lohrke rarely spoke about his baseball career. He once went on a group fishing trip with his son-in-law James. On the drive to the marina, Jack asked James not to bring up the fact that he played in the majors. The anonymous ex-ballplayer then proceeded to haul in one of the biggest catches of the day while flashing an enormous smile.

Though he was quiet and unpretentious about his baseball career, Lohrke was even more restrained in discussing his World War II service and his two months with the Spokane Indians, even among family and close friends. He preferred to keep the painful memories close to the vest. On rare occasions, he granted interviews about the bus crash, albeit reluctantly. In 1994, sportswriter Ron Fimrite wrote a story about the 1946 Spokane Indians for *Sports Illustrated.* After multiple requests, Lohrke finally agreed to an interview but kept his comments brief. When asked about the nickname forced upon him, Lohrke said, "I'll tell you this: nobody out of baseball calls me Lucky Lohrke these days. I may have been lucky, but the name is Jack. Jack Lohrke."[17]

Seven years later, Seattle hosted Major League Baseball's All-Star game, and the Pacific Northwest enjoyed a rare moment as the center of baseball attention. CNN ran a feature about the bus crash to coincide with the festivities, and Lohrke shared his memories on camera. True to form, he answered a reporter's questions with as few words as possible. Lohrke described learning about his promotion to San Diego in Ellensburg and notifying his parents that he was alive. "A road trip in the forties was something else," he said as his eyes welled up.[18] Fifty-five years had passed, but the recollections remained painful.

Jack Lohrke gained the perspective of a life well-lived in the decades following his brief experience in Spokane, but his teammates from the 1946 Indians were never forgotten. "When you're the age I was back then, you haven't a care in the world," he told *Sports Illustrated.* "You're playing ball because you want to play—and they're giving you money to do it. And then . . . well, sometimes those names spring back at me."[19]

The names were Freddie Martinez, Chris Hartje, George Risk, Bob James, Mel Cole, Bob Kinnaman, George Lyden, Bob Paterson, and Vic Picetti.

EPILOGUE

Like Jack Lohrke, the other Spokane Indians who skirted death in 1946 lived with traumatic memories that lingered through the decades. Forty years after the accident, Milt Cadinha and Gus Hallbourg admitted that they thought of the team often. Dick Powers, on the other hand, coped by suppressing his recollections. "I've just put it out of my mind," he said in 1986. "I don't think about it. It was a sad thing and it's sad to think about, even now."[1] By then, Powers and Hallbourg were the last remaining of the six crash survivors. Powers died in 2001 at the age of eighty-four; Hallbourg passed away in 2007 at eighty-seven.

Joe Faria, who operated his Stadium Club bar and restaurant for thirty-seven years, died in 1992. His convertible passenger and lifelong friend, Cadinha, passed away a decade later at the age of eighty.

Jack Lohrke died in 2009, two days after suffering a stroke. He was eighty-five.

Dutch Anderson, the team trainer who happened to skip the deadly trip to Bremerton, met Holly Hartje, Chris's wife, at the hospital after the accident. He expressed his condolences and gave Holly $20 that Chris had loaned him.[2] Later, when they were both back home in San Francisco, Dutch and Holly met again through a mutual friend. They began dating and eventually married, raising Chris's daughter, Christine, and a daughter they had together named Caren. Anderson, who received a Purple Heart for his service in World War II, coached baseball at the University of San Francisco from 1954 to 1961 before enjoying a long scouting career with the Cincinnati Reds, Montreal Expos, and San Francisco Giants. The Spokane Indians team photo remained a fixture in the Anderson home. "I see it every day," said Dutch in 1996. "I think about those guys, just getting started in life. They all had high hopes, and the bubble busted."[3] Dutch died in 2005; Holly passed away in 2018 at age one hunderd and two.

Vic Picetti's fiancée, Betty, eventually married Ronnie King, who played in the minor leagues and then scouted for the Pittsburgh Pirates and Los Angeles Dodgers. King signed or helped develop such notable players as Steve Sax, Bob Oliver, Max Venable, and Greg Vaughn. Ironically, it was Vic who had introduced Betty to Ronnie when Ronnie was a visiting clubhouse attendant for the Sacramento Solons in 1945.

Bob Paterson's sister, Dorothy Tobin, lived to be ninety-five. Her brother's death left her with a sadness that she carried until the day she died. Dorothy loved to talk about her only sibling, but doing so usually left her in tears regardless of the number of years that had passed. Her four children—Cathy, Colleen, Robert, and Myles—always felt like Uncle Bob was a part of the family, even though they never got the chance to know him.[4] They treasure photographs of their tall, handsome relative and have an original copy of his Oakland Oaks contract, which they happened across online.

Ferris Field was heavily damaged by a fire in October 1948 and rebuilt with steel, concrete, and bench-style seats. The Indians' poor play, uncomfortable bleachers, and the expansion of television contributed to a sharp decline in attendance during the next decade. In 1951, the Indians went bare kneed on Sundays, wearing shorts in an effort to lure fans. The club needed much more than Veeckian stunts to keep from going under, however. In 1956, the franchise, now community owned, went bankrupt. A year later, Spokane had no professional baseball for the first time since World War II.

When the Brooklyn Dodgers moved west to Los Angeles in 1958, Spokane was chosen as the new home of their Triple A affiliate. To accommodate the Pacific Coast League team, Spokane County built a new ballpark, now known as Avista Stadium. In fourteen seasons as the Dodgers' top farm club, Spokane was home to some of the greatest minor league teams ever assembled. The standout 1970 squad, managed by Tommy Lasorda, was named the greatest minor league team of the last fifty years by *Baseball America* in 1993. The roster was full of future big leaguers, including Bill Buckner, Steve Garvey, Bobby Valentine, Tom Paciorek, Davey Lopes, Bill Russell, Doyle Alexander, Charlie Hough, and Geoff Zahn.

From 1973 to 1982, Spokane served as home to the Texas Rangers' Triple A affiliate. Since 1983, the Indians have played in Class A circuits. When the minor leagues were restructured by Major League Baseball in 2021, the Indians became a member of the High A Northwest League in the Colorado Rockies' chain. In 1985, the team was purchased by major leaguers George and Ken Brett, and their brothers, John and Bobby.

Dwight Aden served as the team's business manager for only one season, but he remained a staple in Spokane for the rest of his life. When the Indians held a centennial celebration in 2003, Aden threw out the ceremonial first pitch. Four years later, the Spokane Indians established a Rim of Honor at Avista Stadium and inducted Aden and Levi McCormack as two of the four permanent members; the others are Lasorda and Maury Wills.

When the park now known as Avista Stadium was built, it had teepee ticket booths. In the early 1960s, the Spokane players wore headdresses with feathers to opening day galas.[5] Advertisements for upcoming games in the local papers included a depiction of a Native American in headdress and face paint. Times were different.

In 1968, the National Congress of American Indians, representing hundreds of tribal nations, began a campaign to confront the use of derogatory and harmful Native American stereotypes in popular culture, media, and sports. The organization has expressed that "unsanctioned sports mascots are symbols of disrespect that degrade, mock, and harm Native people, particularly Native youth."[6] In the 1970s, several universities across the country retired Native American mascots, including Stanford University, which dropped the name Indians following student-led protests.

In the late 1980s, Charlene Teters, a member of the Spokane Tribe who was enrolled in a graduate program at the University of Illinois at Urbana-Champaign, attended a basketball game and witnessed a disturbing halftime performance by the school's mascot, Chief Illiniwek. She began to lead protests against the mascot and later helped found the National Coalition on Racism in Sports and in the Media. "Native Americans are the only race still relegated to the role of a mascot," Teters told the *New York Times* in 1989. "It makes you feel bad and you're not sure why."[7]

In the early 1990s, the National Education Association passed resolutions denouncing the use of ethnic-related sports team mascots, symbols, and team names. As protests grew louder, the Spokane Indians in 1993 adopted a dinosaur as the team's mascot and removed Native American logos and images. In the years since, many college and professional sports teams have followed suit. Eighteen years after Teters's initial protests, the University of Illinois retired Chief Illiniwek.

The Cleveland Indians franchise changed its name to the Guardians in 2021. The Spokane Baseball Club, on the other hand, maintains the Indians name, but only after consultation and collaboration with the Spokane Tribal Council. In 2006, the team engaged with the tribe and volunteered to drop the team name. Tribe elders supported keeping it and encouraged the team to instead use it as a means of educating the community. The two sides partnered to create a pair of logos honoring the Spokane Tribe; one is an *S* with eagle feathers and the other is a shoulder patch with "Spokane Indians Baseball Club" written in Salish, the tribe's native dialect. It was the first example of a Native American language appearing on a professional baseball uniform.[8] The logos were unveiled on November 29, 2006, during a ceremony at the Northwest Museum of Arts and Culture. Since then, the baseball club and tribe have partnered to pursue ongoing educational and charitable initiatives. In 2014, the team unveiled home jerseys emblazoned with *Sp'q'n'i*, which is Spokane in the Salish language. The jersey is displayed at the National Baseball Hall of Fame in Cooperstown, New York. Signage in Avista Stadium is written in English and Salish, and an exhibit just outside the ballpark entrance describes the traditions of the Spokane Tribe. The team also has added another mascot—a redband trout that represents a historically important source of food for the native people.

On June 23, 2023—seventy-seven years to the day after the 1946 Spokane Indians played their last game—a friend and I watched the present-day iteration take on the Tri-City Dust Devils at Avista Stadium. In many ways, our experience vastly differed from games at Ferris Field in 1946. In between innings, the stadium speakers blasted the music of Taylor Swift while fans angled to catch T-shirts launched by a giant slingshot. A mascot named

"Ribby the Redband Trout" performed a gyrating dance to the delight of the crowd. A pitch clock ensured that the game moved along at a pace quick enough to prevent spectators from being distracted by smartphones. Many aspects of the game, however, remain virtually unchanged. The ballpark still emanates the familiar aroma of popcorn and hot dogs. A run-scoring triple, capped off with a headfirst dive into third base, is still one of the most exciting plays in the game. And players and managers continue to gripe about the strike zone. After all these years, the umpires are still taking heat, and the Spokane roster remains full of talented young ballplayers with dreams of playing in the big leagues.

The next day, I woke up and drove west across Washington. I passed Ritzville, Moses Lake, and Ellensburg, then made it to Snoqualmie Pass. Part of the old Sunset Highway, now known as Forest Service Road 58, remains intact just west of the pass. Old growth forest covers the mountainside below the road except for one area that is strewn with boulders. Nearby, there are remnants of downed concrete posts and guard wire. As I peered down the ravine, I thought of the sixteen men on the bus and the trauma they experienced on that early summer day so many years ago. Then I trekked back to my car and carried on.

ACKNOWLEDGMENTS

Numerous people shared insights and information that helped bring this story to life, and I can't thank them enough.

I am truly grateful to John Lohrke, James McGee, and Karen Kaiser for providing stories of Jack Lohrke's life and career.

Thank you to Leslie Thorgeirson and Lynn Dowd for your hospitality and for making Vic Picetti's letters, mementos, and photos available. Likewise, I appreciate Colleen Finney's willingness to share Bob Paterson's personal letters and family memories.

Gratitude is due to several other descendants of the players involved in this story. Though Robert Picetti was too young to remember his brother when he died, he provided helpful information about his family. Caren Sutton shared photos and information about Chris Hartje and John "Dutch" Anderson. Alex Barisoff and Robert Barisoff took the time to talk about their father and uncle, respectively. Paul Kane communicated about his father, Irv Konopka. Alicia Hicks and Jessica Hicks provided helpful information and articles related to the life of Bob James. Ray Geraghty spent time discussing his Uncle Ben. Sharon Lyden shared details about George Lyden. Lisa Johnson provided awesome photos and information about Bob Kinnaman. Megan Dean-Turner and Jimmy Powers shared their fond memories of Dick Powers.

I was fortunate to interview several former major leaguers who played for Ben Geraghty more than sixty years ago: Howie Bedell, John DeMerit, Tommy John, Ted Kazanski, and Gordy Lund. Felix Mantilla Jr. served as an intermediary between his father and me. Joe Morgan shared his memories of Ben with a handwritten letter.

Many thanks to Pacific Northwest baseball historian David Eskenazi for providing photos from his personal collection. Additional appreciation to the Jacksonville Jumbo Shrimp for sharing a photograph of Henry Aaron and Ben Geraghty.

For research assistance with Jack Lohrke's 216th Field Artillery Battalion, appreciation goes to Bill Beigel of WW2 Research Inc. Additional thanks to the Spokane Public Library, National Baseball Hall of Fame, King County Archives, and Spokane County Superior Court Clerk's Office for providing research materials.

Thank you to accomplished author Bill Nowlin for taking the time to read the manuscript and provide feedback.

Additional gratitude to retired *Spokesman-Review* sportswriter Jim Price for reviewing the book and providing suggestions. Jim is the foremost authority on baseball history in Spokane, and it was an honor to have his input.

I am grateful to Christen Karniski, Andrew Yoder, and the team at Rowman & Littlefield for giving me the opportunity to turn a Word document on my laptop into a book. They were delightful to work with throughout the process.

As always, I thank my family for their unending support, including my wife and best friend, Gina, parents, Barb and Mike Edler, and mother-in-law, Karen Bonacorsi. I would be remiss not to also mention my trusty four-legged writing companions: Bandit, Ralphie, and Edgar.

Finally, a shout-out to my good friend and fellow baseball fanatic, Jonathan Hall, who flew across the country and accompanied me on a road trip to Spokane as we retraced the journey of the 1946 Spokane Indians and experienced present-day baseball in eastern Washington.

NOTES

PROLOGUE

1. Gary Bedingfield, "When Baseball Went to War," in *When Baseball Went to War*, ed. Todd Anton and Bill Nowlin (Chicago: Triumph Books, 2008), 14.

2. The book *Who's on First: Replacement Players in World War II*, published in 2015 by the Society for American Baseball Research, chronicles the impact that World War II had on each Major League team and includes bios of players who debuted during the war.

CHAPTER 1

1. "Injuries Mar Eastsiders' Third Victory," *Pasadena Post*, March 18, 1940, 6.

2. Craig Muder, "President Roosevelt Gives 'Green Light' to Baseball," https://baseballhall.org/discover/inside-pitch/roosevelt-sendsgreen-light-letter, accessed June 3, 2023.

3. Monroe McConnell, "S.D. Wins, 6–1, then Loses, 3–1," *San Diego Union*, March 16, 1942, 11.

4. Monroe McConnell, "The Score Board," *San Diego Union*, March 22, 1942, 53.

5. Monroe McConnell, "The Score Board," *San Diego Union*, April 19, 1942, 51.

6. *Presenting the 35th Infantry Division in World War II, 1941–1945* (Albert Love Enterprises, 1946), chapter 1, https://worldwartwoveterans.org/wp-content/

uploads/2020/09/35th-Infantry-Division-Unit-History-PDF-Book.pdf, accessed May 20, 2023.

7. *Presenting the 35th Infantry Division in World War II, 1941–1945*, chapter 2.

8. 216th Field Artillery Battalion, Battery A Company Morning Report, July 7, 1944.

9. Antony Beevor, *Ardennes 1944: The Battle of the Bulge* (New York: Penguin Random House, 2015), 238.

10. *Presenting the 35th Infantry Division in World War II, 1941–1945*, chapter 10.

11. James McGee, *The Baseball Odyssey: Volume 1—Jack Lohrke* (Small Miracles Publishing Company, 2020).

12. Robert Weintraub, *The Victory Season: The End of World War II and the Birth of Baseball's Golden Age* (New York: Hachette, 2013), 141.

13. Beevor, *Ardennes 1944*, 364.

14. Beevor, *Ardennes 1944*, 367.

15. "Stewart Fired One of Closing Shots at Nazis," *Bradenton Herald*, June 25, 1945, 3.

16. Dedication of Santa Fe Stadium Official Program, July 1, 1945, www.coulthart.com/134/santa-fe-stadium.pdf, accessed July 31, 2023.

17. Al Del Greco, "At Random in Sportdom," *Bergen Evening Record*, August 11, 1945, 9.

18. John Steadman, "46 Years Ago, Ballplayer Really Was 'Lucky,'" *Daily Press*, May 23, 1992, 6.

19. Ron Fimrite, "O Lucky Man," *Sports Illustrated*, November 14, 1994, https://vault.si.com/vault/1994/11/14/o-lucky-man-a-twist-of-fate-saved-jack-lohrke-from-the-worst-tragedy-in-minor-league-history.

20. New York, U.S., Arriving Passenger and Crew Lists, September 10, 1945, www.ancestry.com/imageviewer/collections/7488/images/NYT715_7001-0795, accessed February 28, 2023.

21. Reports of the plane crash have varied over the years. Some reports said the plane crashed after takeoff from New Jersey and other articles stated that the plane crashed in Ohio. Bill King, "Braves Grab Lucky Lohrke," *Evening World-Herald*, August 16, 1946, 26, cited that the crash occurred in Kansas City. The dates and details of the crash align with when Lohrke would have traveled.

22. "20 Returned Veterans Die in Air Crash," *Tampa Tribune*, September 16, 1945, 4.

23. "Lohrke Stars as Locals Turn in 14 to 5 Triumph," *Metropolitan Pasadena Star-News*, September 24, 1945, 16.

CHAPTER 2

1. Gremp and Sain were among the players who enrolled in a rigorous naval preflight pilot training program, where they would suit up with Ted Williams on a team called the Cloudbusters, which is chronicled in Anne R. Keene's book, *The Cloudbuster Nine*.

2. Jeffrey Kurz, "When Choate Was the Home of the Braves," February 24, 2009, https://baseballhall.org/discover/inside-pitch/roosevelt-sendsgreen-light-letter, accessed April 13, 2023.

3. Roger Birtwell, "Nanny Going into Army; Stengel in Gloomy Mood," *Boston Globe*, March 23, 1943, 26.

4. Birtwell, "Nanny Going into Army; Stengel in Gloomy Mood."

5. "Killed by Trucks," *Asbury Park Press*, August 4, 1926, 13.

6. "Trio of School Aces and Three Prepsters Named on Honor Team," *Courier-News*, March 26, 1932, 16.

7. Bill McCullough, "Young Collegian Proves Standout of Citrus Circuit," *Brooklyn Times-Union*, March 30, 1936, 11.

8. "Wildcats Catching Owls at Right Time," *Philadelphia Inquirer*, March 1, 1935, 21.

9. "With the Teams in Training," *Tampa Times*, March 14, 1936, 7.

10. "Villanova Ace Quits Team as Rumors Rise," *Wilkes-Barre Times Leader*, February 28, 1936, 15.

11. Tommy Holmes, "All Around Playing Ability of Villanova Ace Brings Reward," *Brooklyn Daily Eagle*, March 30, 1936, 20.

12. Holmes, "All Around Playing Ability of Villanova Ace Brings Reward."

13. McCullough, "Young Collegian Proves Standout of Citrus Circuit."

14. Larry Babich, "Greatest? Who Can Argue with Hank Aaron?" *Jersey Journal*, April 10, 1998, 25.

15. Bill McCullough, "Stengel to Use Frey in Centerfield When Geraghty Gets Back," *Brooklyn Times-Union*, May 5, 1936, 13.

16. Stuart Rogers, "Geraghty Thumbed to Dodger Bench," *Daily News*, May 5, 1936, 51.

17. Jack Mann, "Henry Aaron: Bad Man with a Bat," *Boys' Life*, March 1972, 11.

18. Marty Appel, *Casey Stengel: Baseball's Greatest Character* (New York: Doubleday, 2017), 61.

19. Appel, *Casey Stengel*, 143.

20. Roger Birtwell, "Geraghty Steps in Where He Left Off," *Boston Globe*, March 26, 1943, 26.

21. "Ben Geraghty Reinstated," *Brooklyn Daily Eagle*," December 20, 1937, 12.

22. "Geraghty Makes New Attempt to Crash Majors," *Brooklyn Daily Eagle*, April 4, 1943, 26.

23. "Ben Geraghty Hurt," *Morning Call*, July 30, 1939, 15.

24. Roger Birtwell, "Tost Called for Induction Next Tuesday," *Boston Globe*, April 8, 1943, 18.

25. Roger Birtwell, "Cuccinello May Play Third," *Boston Globe*, April 8, 1943, 20.

CHAPTER 3

1. Ed Schoenfeld, "Picetti Family All Ball Fans," *Oakland Tribune*, August 22, 1944, 19.

2. U.S. Federal Naturalization Records, 1843–1999, www.ancestry.com/discoveryui-content/view/2920937:3998, accessed March 2, 2023.

3. Bill Leiser, "Picetti Hopes to Graduate into Majors," *San Francisco Chronicle*, June 29, 1944, 13.

4. Leiser, "Picetti Hopes to Graduate into Majors."

5. "Legion Baseball to Continue for Next Year," *San Francisco Chronicle*, December 14, 1942, 16.

6. *San Francisco Chronicle*, June 22, 1944, 15.

7. Ralph Berger, "Dolph Camilli," Society for American Baseball Research BioProject, https://sabr.org/bioproj/person/Dolph-Camilli/, accessed February 22, 2023.

8. Richard Goldstein, "Dolph Camilli, Who Led Dodgers to '41 Pennant, Dies at 90," *New York Times*, October 22, 1997, A25.

9. Bill Leiser, "Vic Picetti Proves up As Finest Young Ball Player in These Parts," *San Francisco Chronicle*, June 27, 1944, 15.

10. Bill Leiser, "30 Baseball Boys Compete for a New Honor That Isn't Empty Friday in Battle of All Stars," *San Francisco Chronicle*, June 21, 1944, 15.

11. Will Connolly, "Picetti Gets All Star Berth," *San Francisco Chronicle*, June 27, 1944, 17.

12. Leiser, "Vic Picetti Proves up As Finest Young Ball Player in These Parts."

13. Leiser, "Vic Picetti Proves up As Finest Young Ball Player in These Parts."

14. Leiser, "Vic Picetti Proves up As Finest Young Ball Player in These Parts."

15. Leiser, "Picetti Hopes to Graduate into Majors."

16. Bill Leiser, "As Bill Leiser Sees It," *San Francisco Chronicle*, August 22, 1944, 13.

17. Bob Stevens, "Mission Whiz Kid Joins Acorns in Los Angeles," *San Francisco Chronicle*, August 16, 1944, 13.

18. Al Warden, "Patrolling the Sport Highway," *Ogden Standard-Examiner*, July 29, 1944, 3.

19. "Ashburn Cinches Starting Job for West in All-Star Kid Classic," *Evening World-Herald*, August 5, 1944, 9.

20. Bill Leiser, "Picetti Reunited with Old Pal," *San Francisco Chronicle*, August 2, 1944, 12.

21. Bill Leiser "Ira Thomas, Famous Philadelphia Scout, Tells Picetti That He's a Power Hitter," *San Francisco Chronicle*, August 3, 1944, 12.

22. Bill Leiser, "Picetti Will Bat in Cleanup Spot," *San Francisco Chronicle*, August 5, 1944, 11.

23. Bill Leiser, "35,000 Anticipated Today for All-America Boys' Game in Polo Grounds," *San Francisco Chronicle*, August 7, 1944, 13.

24. Leiser, "Picetti Will Bat in Cleanup Spot."

25. Bill Leiser, "Picetti and His Pal, Roger Brown, Are in Mel Ott's Starting Lineup Tomorrow." *San Francisco Chronicle*, August 6, 1944, 24.

26. Leiser, "Picetti and His Pal, Roger Brown, Are in Mel Ott's Starting Lineup Tomorrow."

27. Leiser, "Picetti Will Bat in Cleanup Spot."

28. Bill Leiser, "Picetti Delivers at Typewriter," *San Francisco Chronicle*, August 11, 1944, 13.

29. Louis Effrat, "East's Nine Wins in Boys' Game, 6–0," *New York Times*, August 8, 1944, 12.

30. Bill Leiser, "Vic Meets Mama and Papa Three Hours Late," *San Francisco Chronicle*, August 13, 1944, 26.

31. Bill Leiser, "Vic Picetti Blasts out Single, Double before 17,803 Fans," *San Francisco Chronicle*, August 8, 1944, 13.

32. Lee Dunbar, "On the Level," *Oakland Tribune*, August 19, 1944, 19.

33. Leiser, "Picetti Delivers at Typewriter."

34. Emmons Byrne, "Yanks Scout Sings Praises of Young Acorn Vic Picetti," *Oakland Tribune*, January 7, 1945, 14.

35. Dunbar, "On the Level."

36. Bill Leiser, "Picetti's Signing Was Inevitable," *San Francisco Chronicle*, August 17, 1944, 13.

37. Dunbar, "On the Level."

38. Schoenfeld, "Picetti Family All Ball Fans."

39. Leiser, "Picetti's Signing Was Inevitable."

40. Leiser, "Picetti's Signing Was Inevitable."

41. Bob Stevens, "Mission Whiz Kid Joins Acorns in Los Angeles," *San Francisco Chronicle*, August 16, 1944, 13.

42. Leiser, "As Bill Leiser Sees It."

43. George Scherck, "Youth Stars As Oakland, Angels Split," *Oakland Tribune*, August 17, 1944, 23.

44. Leiser, "As Bill Leiser Sees It."

45. Correspondence from Hillerich & Bradsby Company to Vic Picetti, November 17, 1944.

46. Emmons Byrne, "Pirate Scout Says Picetti Coast Loop's Best Prospect," *Oakland Tribune*, September 1, 1944, 21.

47. Emmons Byrne, "The Bull Pen," *Oakland Tribune*, December 13, 1944, 11.

48. "Sam Gibson to Pitch against Joe Gordon in Doyle Game," *Press-Democrat*, February 28, 1945, 4.

49. Emmons Byrne, "The Bull Pen," *Oakland Tribune*, February 6, 1945, 11.

50. Angela Picetti, letter to Vic Picetti, postmarked March 8, 1945.

51. Clyde Giraldo, "Acorns Pick Stromme to Duel Bevo's Liska," *San Francisco Chronicle*, March 31, 1945, 11.

52. Harry Borba, "Side Lines," *San Francisco Examiner*, April 24, 1945, 20.

53. Vic Picetti, letter to Victor and Angela Picetti, March 9, 1945.

54. Lee Dunbar, "On the Level," *Oakland Tribune*, May 2, 1945, 16.

55. Emmons Byrne, "Dolph Tells Why He's Benched," *Oakland Tribune*, April 8, 1945, 18.

56. "Tiger Tales," *Bessemer Herald*, May 4, 1945, 4.

57. Vic Picetti, letter to Angela Picetti, postmarked April 11, 1945.

58. Noel Hynd, "The Inside Story about Baseball in 1943 Was Less Bounce to the Ounce," *Sports Illustrated*, May 13, 1985, 130.

59. Dick Dobbins, *The Grand Minor League: An Oral History of the Old Pacific Coast League* (Emeryville, CA: Woodford Press, 1999), 288.

60. Dobbins, *The Grand Minor League*, 28.

61. Dobbins, *The Grand Minor League*, 123.

62. "Dolph Camilli Will Play for Boston Sox," *San Francisco Chronicle*, June 17, 1945, 20.

63. Jim Price, email to the author, August 30, 2023.

64. Dolph Camilli, letter to Vic Picetti, July 12, 1945, from Picetti family scrapbook.

65. Lee Dunbar, "On the Level," *Oakland Tribune*, September 28, 1945, 26.

CHAPTER 4

1. Jim Kaplan, "Lefty Grove," Society for American Baseball Research BioProject, https://sabr.org/bioproj/person/Lefty-Grove/, accessed July 3, 2023.

2. Kaplan, "Lefty Grove."

3. Fred Glueckstein, "Tony Lazzeri," Society for American Baseball Research BioProject, https://sabr.org/bioproj/person/tony-lazzeri/, accessed July 3, 2023.

4. Gary Bedingfield, "Baseball in World War II," www.baseballinwartime.com/baseball_in_wwii/baseball_in_wwii.htm, accessed July 15, 2023.

5. Jim Price, "Birth of the Indians," *Spokesman-Review*, June 21, 2003, 64.

6. "Would Help This League," *Spokane Chronicle*, April 23, 1903, 9.

7. Mike Lynch, "Phil Douglas," Society for American Baseball Research BioProject, https://sabr.org/bioproj/person/phil-douglas/, accessed July 10, 2023.

8. "Owner Ulrich Changes Name of Spokane's Baseball Team from 'Hawks' to the 'Indians,'" *Spokane Chronicle*, March 17, 1939, 22.

9. "From the Bench," *Spokane Chronicle*, November 12, 1938, 19.

10. Herb Ashlock, "Collins New Co-Owner of Baseball Club Here," *Spokane Chronicle*, August 18, 1945, 9.

11. "Council O.K.s Contract Shift," *Spokesman-Review*, October 9, 1945, 17.

12. "Victoria Joins W.I. Baseball," *Spokane Chronicle*, September 17, 1945, 13.

13. As of 2023, there have been only fifteen unassisted triple plays in major league history.

14. Denny Spellecy, "Three Teams Agree to Send Players to Spokane Indians," *Spokesman-Review*, December 17, 1945, 3.

15. "Ball Club Owner in Sacred Heart," *Spokane Chronicle*, January 21, 1946, 12.

16. Bob Johnson, "Aden Business Manager of Indians," *Spokane Chronicle*, February 26, 1946, 11.

17. *Spokesman-Review*, October 10, 1935, 13.

18. *Spokane Indians: A Century of Baseball*, directed by Mark Mohr (Peak Video Productions, 2003).

19 "Outfield Star in Fold Again," *Spokesman-Review*, March 3, 1946, 21.

20. "Pasco Ball Team to Disband," *Tacoma News Tribune*, July 10, 1943, 14.

21. "Levi McCormack in Spokane Following Naval Discharge," *Spokesman-Review*, December 20, 1945, 12.

CHAPTER 5

1. Emmons Byrne, "Former Major League Boss Gets $12,000," *Oakland Tribune*, October 17, 1945, 16.

2. Emmons Byrne, "Oakland Prep Star Signed by Detroit for Big Bonus," *Oakland Tribune*, February 8, 1946, 17.

3. Alan Ward, "Patterson's [*sic*] Single Wins 2–1 Battle," *Oakland Tribune*, March 4, 1946, 10.

4. Alan Ward, "On Second Thought," *Oakland Tribune*, March 4, 1946, 10.

5. Bob Paterson's National Association of Professional Baseball Leagues Uniform Player's Contract, provided by Colleen Finney.

6. "Salt Lakers Lose, 7–5, to Russets," *Salt Lake Tribune*, July 18, 1942, 22.

7. Bob Paterson, letter to his family, July 18, 1942; some content removed.

8. "Batting and Pitching," *Post-Register*, August 4, 1942, 6.

9. Bob Paterson, letter to his family, August 1942.

10. Paterson, letter to his family, August 1942.

11. Paterson, letter to his family, August 1942.

12. "Service All-Stars in Game Tomorrow," *Oakland Tribune*, June 4, 1943, 32.

13. Bob Paterson described the home run in a September 1942 letter to his family. The attendance and opposing pitcher was derived from "Surf Riders Win over Preflights by 10 to 9," *Stockton Evening and Sunday Record*, August 7, 1944, 10.

14. "4 Pre-Flight Aces on All-Star Club," *San Francisco Examiner*, September 8, 1944, 18.

15. Bob Paterson, American Baseball Bureau Publicity Questionnaire, March 18, 1946, www.ancestry.com/discoveryui-content/view/19650:61599, accessed April 3, 2023.

16. Ward, "Patterson's [*sic*] Single Wins 2–1 Battle."

17. Alan Ward, "Price Makes Hit at Acorn Spring Camp," *Oakland Tribune*, March 8, 1946, 10.

18. Emmons Byrne, "Oak Hurler Scores Casey for Action," *Oakland Tribune*, May 14, 1946, 24.

19. "W.S.C. Pitcher for Twin Falls," *Spokesman-Review*, August 23, 1939, 29.

20. Dan Walton, "Sports Log," *Tacoma News Tribune*, March 20, 1942, 26.

21. Herb Ashlock, "From the Bench," *Spokane Chronicle*, August 8, 1941, 11.

22. Emmons Byrne, "Much-Sought Army Hurler Becomes Oak," *Oakland Tribune*, January 18, 1946, 16.

23. Herb Ashlock, "From the Bench," *Spokane Chronicle*, June 9, 1942, 11.

24. Ashlock, "From the Bench," June 9, 1942.

25. Funeral Is Set for Tempe Man," *Arizona Republic*, June 28, 1946, 22.

26. "Big League Scouts Watched These Birds," *Arizona Republic*, August 18, 1940, 25.

27. "New Outfielder Slams Homers as Indians Groom for Season," *Spokane Chronicle*, April 4, 1946, 24.

28. "Tempe Athlete Dies in Wreck," *Tucson Daily Citizen*, June 25, 1946, 8.

29. "Tribe Bothered by Wild Running," *Spokesman-Review*, April 21, 1946, 24.

30. Walt Little, "Teamwork Big Indian Problem; Victoria Team Looks Ragged," *Spokane Chronicle*, April 20, 1946, 9.

31. "The History of the Spokane Tribe of Indians," https://spokanetribe.com/history/, accessed July 15, 2023.

32. Don Popejoy and Penny Hutten, *Images of America: Early Spokane* (Charleston, SC: Arcadia, 2010), 7.

33. "The History of the Spokane Tribe of Indians."

34. "Spokane: 1871–1941: A Glance over the Past, a Glimpse of the Present, a Hint of the Future," *Spokesman-Review*, January 26, 1941, 50.

CHAPTER 6

1. Bob Johnson, "Catcher Mel Cole Given Chance As Spokane Team Manager," *Spokane Chronicle*, April 26, 1946, 13.

2. Melvin Chester Cole in the U.S., World War II Navy Muster Rolls, 1938–1949, www.ancestry.com/discoveryui-content/view/32233314:1143, accessed March 26, 2023.

3. "Former Teammates Will Carry Cole's Body," *Sacramento Bee*, June 27, 1946, 22.

4. "Cole Is One of the Youngest Players on El Paso Team," *El Paso Herald-Post*, April 13, 1937, 8.

5. "Candini Near Shutout in 15th Win," *El Paso Herald-Post*, August 6, 1937, 12.

6. Wilbur Adams, "Between the Sport Lines," *Sacramento Bee*, January 1945, 14.

7. Mel Cole, American Baseball Bureau Publicity Questionnaire, January 2, 1946, www.ancestry.com/discoveryui-content/view/95999:61599, accessed March 28, 2023.

8. "Catcher Mel Cole Given Chance As Spokane Team Manager," *Spokane Chronicle*, April 26, 1946, 13.

9. "O Lucky Man," *Sports Illustrated*, November 14, 1994, https://vault.si.com/vault/1994/11/14/o-lucky-man-a-twist-of-fate-saved-jack-lohrke-from-the-worst-tragedy-in-minor-league-history.

10. Warren Corbett, "Glenn Wright," Society for American Baseball Research BioProject, https://sabr.org/bioproj/person/glenn-wright/, accessed March 15, 2023.

11. Bill Bigelow, "As Fate Would Have It . . . ," *Bend Bulletin*, July 16, 2006.

12. Bob Johnson, "Hallbourg Pitching Tonight; Indians Nip Vancouver, 5–0," *Spokane Chronicle*, April 27, 1946, 7.

13. "Dunham Quits on Series Eve," *Spokesman-Review*, April 30, 1946, 8.

14. Robert Weintraub, *The Victory Season: The End of World War II and the Birth of Baseball's Golden Age* (New York: Hachette, 2013), 100.

15. Vic Picetti, letter to Angela Picetti, postmarked May 1, 1946.

16. *Spokane Chronicle*, May 14, 1946, 13.

17. *Spokane Chronicle*, May 14, 1946, 13.

18. David Row, "Kearns Eagles to Field Team," *Deseret News*, March 23, 1945, 14.

19. "Fandom Saw Stars under Fake Names," *Evening Sun*, March 20, 1946, 8.

20. "George Risk Signs with Yankees," *Salt Lake Tribune*, January 15, 1946, 12.

21. Bob Johnson, "My Nickel's Worth," *Spokane Chronicle*, June 27, 1946, 10.

22. "Sport Rays," *Bellingham Herald*, May 26, 1946, 14.

23. Vic Picetti, letter to Angela Picetti, postmarked May 14, 1946.

24. Bob Johnson, "My Nickel's Worth," *Spokane Chronicle*, May 28, 1946, 13.

25. "Standings Tight among First Six in W.I. Circuit," *Spokane Chronicle*, May 22, 1946, 15.

26. Keith Matthews, "Caps Scalp Indians with Smashing 19-Run Barrage," *Vancouver Sun*, May 23, 1946, 7.

27. Alf Cottrell, "Indian Cole Performs War Dance," *Vancouver Sun*, May 25, 1946, 7.

28. "Cole Ousted As Caps in Double Win," *Vancouver Sun*, May 25, 1946, 7.

29. Holman C. Bass obituary, *Modesto Bee*, October 3, 1983, 2.

30. Holman Cray Bass World War II draft card, www.ancestry.com/discovery ui-content/view/10886922:2238, accessed April 4, 2023.

31. *Spokane Chronicle*, May 21, 1946, 13.

32. Bob Johnson, "Spokane Bats Still Booming, Risk Tops Hitters with .378," *Spokane Chronicle*, May 27, 1946, 15.

33. Johnson, "My Nickel's Worth," *Spokane Chronicle*, May 28, 1946, 13.

34. Johnson, "Spokane Bats Still Booming, Risk Tops Hitters with .378."

35. "Victoria Victim of Odd Errors," *Spokesman-Review*, May 30, 1946, 10.

36. Bob Johnson, "Indians Creep toward Lead; Blast Victoria Team, 14–2," *Spokane Chronicle*, May 30, 1946, 22.

37. Vic Picetti, letter to Angela Picetti, May 30, 1946; some content removed.

38. "First Is Close; Afterpiece Wild," *Spokesman-Review*, May 31, 1946, 16.

39. Indians of California Census Rolls, 1928–1993, www.ancestry.com/imageviewer/collections/61006/images/44715_355939-00432, accessed May 16, 2023.

40. M. Shawn Hennessy, "1944 NAS Kaneohe Klippers vs Pearl Harbor Submarine Base—23rd Game," https://chevronsanddiamonds.wordpress.com/1944-nas-kaneohe-klippers-vs-pearl-harbor-submarine-base-23rd-game/, accessed August 5, 2023.

CHAPTER 7

1. "James Pounds Rival Hurlers," *Spokesman-Review*, June 3, 1946, 15.

2. Bob Johnson, "Risk Still Leads the Line-up by Wide Margin," *Spokane Chronicle*, June 4, 1946, 13.

3. Bob Johnson, "Fans Go, but Indians Stay to Surprise Tacoma Tigers," *Spokane Chronicle*, June 5, 1946, 13.

4. "Spokane Indians Lead League; Joe Faria to Pitch Tonight," *Spokane Chronicle*, June 6, 1946, 26.

5. Herb Ashlock, "Hope, Bing Wow Big Gallery; Exhibition Match Ends Even," *Spokane Chronicle*, June 7, 1946, 11.

6. "Cadinha Will Pitch Tonight; Hurler Seeks Seventh Victory," *Spokane Chronicle*, June 8, 1946, 17.

7. Vic Picetti, letter to Angela Picetti, June 12, 1946.

8. "Tacoma Tossers Beat Spokane Twice, 11–3 and 5–4; Wenatchee Here This Week," *Tacoma News Tribune*, June 18, 1946, 10.

9. "Humbled Indians Returning Home to Meet Salem," *Spokane Chronicle*, June 17, 1946, 13.

10. "Spokane Indians Will Meet Salem in Vital Series," *Spokane Chronicle*, June 18, 1946, 13.

11. Bob Johnson, "Score Umpires for Poor Work; Spokane-Salem Series Is Even," *Spokane Chronicle*, June 22, 1946, 17.

12. "Pros Draft 3 Vandal Stars," *Times-News*, April 9, 1943, 6.

13. "The Blues Get Hartje," *Kansas City Star*, April 5, 1938, 12; "Food Makes Blues Ill," *Kansas City Times*, June 6, 1938, 2.

14. "Hartje's Mother Is Dead," *Kansas City Star*, July 7, 1938, 10; "Silvestri to Replace Hartje against Tribe," *Indianapolis Star*, July 10, 1938, 19.

15. Bob Ray, "Oakland Errors Pave Way for Stars' 9–5 Victory," *Los Angeles Times*, August 4, 1938, 28.

16. Hy Turkin, "Dodgers Spend $50,000 for 3 Yank Farmhands," *Daily News*, February 7, 1939, 247.

17. Harold Parrott, "Basque Second Sacker No Longer Tabbed As 'Nice-Nelly' Ball Player," *Brooklyn Daily Eagle*, September 15, 1939, 18.

18. Marc T. McNeil, "Royals Buy Chris Hartje from Dodgers, Obtain Bert Haas on Option," *Montreal Gazette*, April 23, 1940, 14.

19. "Chris Hartje Iron Man in Mask for Royals," *Montreal Star*, August 3, 1939, 21.

20. Parrott, "Basque Second Sacker No Longer Tabbed As 'Nice-Nelly' Ball Player."

21. Parrott, "Basque Second Sacker No Longer Tabbed As 'Nice-Nelly' Ball Player."

22. McNeil, "Royals Buy Chris Hartje from Dodgers, Obtain Bert Haas on Option."

23. Marc T. McNeil, "A Changed Man," *Montreal Gazette*, June 24, 1941, 14.

24. "Chris Hartje Is Homesick," *Montreal Daily Star*, May 30, 1940, 35.

25. McNeil, "A Changed Man."

26. Caren Sutton, interview with the author, February 24, 2023.

27. "Spokane Defense Tight; Offense Falls to Pieces," *Spokane Chronicle*, June 20, 1946, 12.

28. "Hurler Cadinha in Rare Fettle at Ferris Field," *Spokane Chronicle*, June 21, 1946, 11.

29. "Five-Run First Aids Salem Win," *Spokesman-Review*, June 22, 1946, 9.

30. Vic Picetti, letter to Angela Picetti, June 21, 1946; some content removed.

31. Ron Fimrite, "O Lucky Man," *Sports Illustrated*, November 14, 1994, https://vault.si.com/vault/1994/11/14/o-lucky-man-a-twist-of-fate-saved-jack-lohrke-from-the-worst-tragedy-in-minor-league-history.

32. "Spokane Wins Salem Series, 4–3," *Spokesman-Review*, June 24, 1946, 7.

33. Bob Johnson, "My Nickel's Worth," *Spokane Chronicle*, June 27, 1946, 10.

34. Bob Johnson, "My Nickel's Worth," *Spokane Chronicle*, August 22, 1946, 26.

35. Bob Johnson, "My Nickel's Worth," *Spokane Chronicle*, July 9, 1946, 11.

36. Johnson, "My Nickel's Worth," June 27, 1946.

37. Howie Stalwick, "I Am the Shadow Sinister Called Fate," *Nashua Telegraph*, June 23, 2003, 11.

CHAPTER 8

1. Bob Johnson, "My Nickel's Worth," *Spokane Chronicle*, February 18, 1956, 8.

2. "Victim's Own Story Varies from Others," *Seattle Star*, June 27, 1946, 1.

3. Jack Lohrke interview on CNN, aired July 7, 2001.

4. Ron Fimrite, "O Lucky Man," *Sports Illustrated*, November 14, 1994, https://vault.si.com/vault/1994/11/14/o-lucky-man-a-twist-of-fate-saved-jack-lohrke-from-the-worst-tragedy-in-minor-league-history.

5. Colin Diltz, "A Glimpse of Washington State's First Highway from Seattle through the Cascades," *Seattle Times*, May 23, 2019, www.seattletimes.com/seattle-news/transportation/a-glimpse-of-washington-states-first-highway-from-seattle-through-the-cascades/, accessed July 8, 2023.

6. "Victim's Own Story Varies from Others," *Seattle Star*, June 27, 1946, 1.

7. "Chartered Bus Plunges off Snoqualmie Pass Grade; Several Are Hurt," *Spokesman-Review*, June 25, 1946, 11.

8. "Victim's Own Story Varies from Others."

9. Jim Price, "A Half-Century of Pain," *Spokesman-Review*, June 24, 1996, 23.

10. Roger Birtwell, "Ex-Brave Geraghty Foiled Death, Lived to Humble Sox," *Boston Globe*, April 5, 1951, 16.

11. "Spokane's Ball Team Hurtled Down an Embankment," *Spokane Chronicle*, June 25, 1946, 5.

12. Birtwell, "Ex-Brave Geraghty Foiled Death, Lived to Humble Sox."

13. "8th Player Succumbs to Crash Hurts," *Seattle Daily Times*, June 25, 1946, 2.

14. Michael Flynn, "Baseball Bus Tragedy of 1946 is Recalled," *Buffalo News*, June 23, 1981, 42.

15. "Bottom Fell from under Us, Says Survivor of Accident," *Seattle Daily Times*, June 25, 1946, 3.

16. Birtwell, "Ex-Brave Geraghty Foiled Death, Lived to Humble Sox."

17. Nelson Allen, "Truck Driver, First as Scene of Bush [*sic*] Crash, Tells Grim Story," *Seattle Star*, June 25, 1946, 5

18. "Bottom Fell from under Us, Says Survivor of Accident."

19. *Seattle Post-Intelligencer*, June 25, 1946, 1.

20. "Chartered Bus Plunges off Snoqualmie Pass Grade; Several Are Hurt."

21. "Chartered Bus Plunges off Snoqualmie Pass Grade; Several Are Hurt."

22. Jerry O'Brien, "Baseball's Darkest Night," *Spokesman-Review*, June 24, 1956, 90.

23. O'Brien, "Baseball's Darkest Night."

24. "Baseball's Darkest Night," *Spokesman-Review*, June 20, 1971, 109.

25. Bob Wolf, "Mr. Lucky," *Los Angeles Times*, June 27, 1990, 200.

26. Jim Price, "Forty Years Later, Ex-Indians Look Back on Spokane's Worst Sports Tragedy," *Spokesman-Review*, June 22, 1986, 32.

27. Wolf, "Mr. Lucky."

28. Wolf, "Mr. Lucky."

29. "Bottom Fell from under Us, Says Survivor of Accident."

30. "8th Player Succumbs to Crash Hurts."

31. "Spokane's Ball Team Hurtled Down an Embankment."

32. "Bottom Fell from Under Us, Says Survivor of Accident."

33. "Victim's Own Story Varies from Others."

34. "George Lyden Eighth Bus Crash Fatality," *Spokesman-Review*, June 26, 1946, 9.

35. "8th Bus Crash Victim Dies," *Seattle Post-Intelligencer*, June 26, 1946, 5.

36. "Chris Hartje Dies; Benefit Games for Families Sought," *San Francisco Chronicle*, June 27, 1946, 17.

37. Alex Shults, "Gun Club Homeless; Devine Started 14 Spokane Players," *Seattle Daily Times*, June 27, 1946, 14.

38. Caren Sutton, interview with the author, February 24, 2023.

39. "Crash Victim, Friend," *Seattle Daily Times*, June 28, 1946, 13.

40. "Bus Crash Probe Waits on Driver," *Seattle Daily Times*, July 2, 1946, 2.

41. "Was Tough Team," *Spokane Chronicle*, June 25, 1946, 13.

42. "Search for Car," *Spokesman-Review*, June 27, 1946, 1.

43. Jim Price, "Dreams of Picetti, Eight Others Ended Six Decades Ago," *Spokesman-Review*, June 18, 2006, 35.

44. Curtis Hammerbeck, letter to Angela Picetti, June 1946, Picetti family scrapbook.

45. "Oaks Mourn Picetti; PCL to Help Spokane," *San Francisco Chronicle*, June 26, 1946, 17.

46. Bill Leiser, "Picetti's Loyalty Couldn't Be Swerved," *San Francisco Chronicle*, June 27, 1946, 17.

47. "A Case of Sportsmanship," *Evening World-Herald*, July 9, 1946, 11.

48. Robert Picetti, interview with the author, March 1, 2023.

49. Wolf, "Mr. Lucky."

CHAPTER 9

1. Ball Clubs to Help Spokane," *Seattle Post-Intelligencer*, June 25, 1946, 17.

2. Bob Miller, "Shattered Team to Play Again," *Spokesman-Review*, June 27, 1946, 28.

3. Bob Johnson, "Proceeds to Aid Kin of Players Dead and Hurt," *Spokane Chronicle*, June 27, 1946, 20.

4. Bob Johnson, "Benefit Association Formed to Aid Kin of Dead Players," *Spokane Chronicle*, June 28, 1946, 11.

5. "Spokane Indians Hold Initial Workout As Rebuilding Begins," *Spokesman-Review*, July 1, 1946, 1.

6. "Benefit Sales Described Low," *Spokesman-Review*, July 4, 1946, 6.

7. Spokane Memorial Baseball program, July 8, 1946.

8. Spokane Memorial Baseball program.

9. Jim Price, "A Half-Century of Pain," *Spokesman-Review*, June 24, 1996, 25.

10. Alex Shults, "Ghosts of Spokane Ball Players Still Roam Park," *Seattle Daily Times*, July 6, 1946, 7.

11. Bob Miller, "Sports in Review," *Spokesman-Review*, July 31, 1946, 20.

12. Bob Miller, "Sam Collins Signs Working Agreement with Dodgers Farm Organization," *Spokesman-Review*, August 1, 1946, 10.

13. Bob Johnson, "My Nickel's Worth," *Spokane Chronicle*, August 22, 1946, 26.

14. "Benefit Fund Nears $70,000," *Spokesman-Review*, July 28, 1946, 21.

15. "Golfers Shoot for Big Prizes," *Spokesman-Review*, July 15, 1946, 7.

16. "Hole-in-One Contest Pays," *Spokesman-Review*, July 31, 1946, 2.

17. Bob Miller, "Sports in Review," *Spokesman-Review*, September 1, 1946, 19.

18. Bob Johnson, "My Nickel's Worth," *Spokane Chronicle*, September 3, 1946, 13.

19. "Cadinha Purchased by the Hollywood Stars," *Spokane Chronicle*, September 10, 1946, 13.

20. Bob Miller, "Sports in Review," *Spokesman-Review*, September 9, 1946, 7.

21. "Victims and Dependents of Baseball Tragedy to Receive $114,805.25," *Spokane Chronicle*, December 20, 1946, 17.

22. Bob Miller, "Sports in Review," *Spokesman-Review*, September 1, 1946, 19.

23. Order approving settlement records was obtained from the Spokane County Superior Court Clerk's Office.

24. Bob Miller, "Sports in Review," *Spokesman-Review*, October 29, 1946, 18.

25. Wolf, "Mr. Lucky."

26. Wolf, "Mr. Lucky."

27. Bob Johnson, "My Nickel's Worth," *Spokane Chronicle*, July 9, 1946, 11.

28. Alf Cottrell, "Backtracking on 'Lucky Lohrke,'" *Vancouver Sun*, February 26, 1947, 11.

29. Bill Bicker, "Jack Lohrke Boomed As All-Time Hot Corner Prospect," *Spokesman-Review*, August 31, 1946, 17.

30. Ken Bojens, "Off the Main Line," *San Diego Union*, November 2, 1946, 15.

31. Wolf, "Mr. Lucky."

32. Bob Johnson, "My Nickel's Worth," *Spokane Chronicle*, August 22, 1946, 26.

33. Wolf, "Mr. Lucky."

34. Mitch Angus, "Final Deal Near Working Pact," *San Diego Union*, December 9, 1946, 13.

35. Wolf, "Mr. Lucky."

CHAPTER 10

1. "Ben Geraghty Has Set up Some High-Flying Goals," *Courier-Journal*, April 16, 1960, 30.

2. Jack Mann, "Braves Have Man for the Job, But . . ." *Newsday*, October 23, 1959, 98.

3. "Ben Geraghty to Be Playing Manager of Indians; Injuries Have Healed," *Spokane Chronicle*, February 4, 1947, 13.

4. Bob Johnson, "McCormack in Good Fettle; Jittery Complex Hits Team," *Spokane Chronicle*, June 19, 1947, 28.

5. Bob Johnson, "My Nickel's Worth," *Spokane Chronicle*, November 13, 1947, 98.

6. Bob Miller, "Most Voluble Owner," *Spokesman-Review*, April 21, 1948, 23.

7. Vince O'Keefe, "Memories of Two Great Gentlemen," *Seattle Daily Times*, September 28, 1974, 9.

8. "Sunday for Injured Hurler," *Oakland Tribune*, January 23, 1947, 25.

9. Flem Hall, "The Sport Tide," *Fort Worth Star-Telegram*, March 25, 1948, 40.

10. Ed Levitt, "He Bagged a Winner with Stadium Club," *Oakland Tribune*, May 8, 1985, 53.

11. Jimmy Powers, interview with the author, May 26, 2023.

12. "Grateful Notes Sent by Wives," *Spokane Chronicle*, January 1, 1947, 15.

13. Megan Dean-Turner, personal communication to the author, Facebook, April 5, 2023.

14. Jim Price, "Berg Lived with Dignity," *Spokesman-Review*, November 2, 2003, 34.

15. James P. Dawson, "Lohrke, Impressive in Giant Drill, Seen Bolstering New York Infield," *New York Times*, February 19, 1947, 32.

16. Al Laney, "Thread of Destiny Led Jack Lohrke to Giants," *The Sporting News*, March 5, 1947, 11.

17. James McGee, interview with the author, March 6, 2023.

CHAPTER 11

1. Bob Quincy, "Aaron 'Host' for All-Stars," *Charlotte Observer*, April 1, 1978, 7.

2. "Geraghty Resigns As Meridian Pilot," *Selma Times-Journal*, June 1, 1948, 8.

3. Gene Thompson, "Looking at Sports," *Bristol Herald Courier*, February 27, 1949, 14.

4. Gene Thompson, "Looking at Sports," *Bristol Herald Courier*, April 23, 1950, 9.

5. Gene Thompson, "Looking at Sports," *Bristol Herald Courier*, April 17, 1950, 6.

6. Thompson, "Looking at Sports," April 17, 1950.

7. Thompson, "Looking at Sports," April 17, 1950.

8. Pat Jordan, *A False Spring* (New York: Dodd, Mead, 1975), 197.

9. Red Harrington, "Geraghty, Twins Arrive Home to Royal Bristol Welcome," *Bristol Herald Courier*, April 25, 1950, 8.

10. "Ben Geraghty Will Manage Jacksonville Next Season," *Bristol Herald Courier*, December 10, 1950, 23.

11. Bill Westwick, "Money Keeps 'Sugar' Haunting Battle Pit," *Ottawa Journal*, June 26, 1963, 15.

12. Henry Aaron and Lonnie Wheeler, *I Had a Hammer: The Hank Aaron Story* (New York: Harper, 1991), 56.

13. Aaron and Wheeler, *I Had a Hammer*, 56.

14. Pete Wevurski, "Clubhouse Journal," *Jersey Journal*, July 10, 1975, 7.

15. Jordan, *A False Spring*, 204.

16. Jordan, *A False Spring*, 203.

17. Aaron and Wheeler, *I Had a Hammer*, 64.

18. Aaron and Wheeler, *I Had a Hammer*, 57.

19. Aaron and Wheeler, *I Had a Hammer*, 58.

20. Félix Mantilla Jr., interview with the author, April 20, 2023.

21. Mantilla Jr., interview.

22. Pete Swanson, "'Hoss' Garner Recalls Aaron's Days in Minors: 'Wonder What Those People Think Now,'" *Evansville Press*, April 14, 1974, 47.

23. Ray Crawford, "Aaron a Long Way from Jacksonville," *Miami Herald*, March 24, 1974, 118.

24. Ray Crawford, "Dedicated to Game, Geraghty Just Couldn't Stand Losing," *Miami Herald*, June 19, 1963, 23.

25. Crawford, "Dedicated to Game, Geraghty Just Couldn't Stand Losing."

26. "Braves Rookie Aaron Slugs Even Bad Balls," *Daily News*, March 27, 1954, 131.

27. Aaron and Wheeler, *I Had a Hammer*, 71.

28. Joel H. Cohen, *Hammerin' Hank of the Braves* (New York: Scholastic Book Services, 1971), 32.

29. Johnny Carrico, "What Magic Brought Colonels First Pennant Since 1946?" *Courier-Journal*, September 13, 1959, 71.

30. Tom Kinney, *Columbus Ledger*, August 7, 1953, 12.

31. Wilton Garrison, "Man Who Wins with Jax Braves Survived Terrible Bus Tragedy," *Charlotte Observer*, April 24, 1954, 8.

32. Bob Quincy, "Lee Hotter Than Palmer," *Charlotte Observer*, May 31, 1954, 20.

33. Garrison, "Man Who Wins with Jax Braves Survived Terrible Bus Tragedy."

34. Gene Thompson, "Looking at Sports," *Bristol Herald Courier*, February 19, 1955, 7.

35. Dick Pierce, "Big League Managers a Fraternal Order—Once in, Who Wants Out?" *Charlotte Observer*, August 3, 1956, 12.

36. *Lake Geneva Regional News*, February 23, 1956, 2.

37. Joe Morgan, letter to the author, March 2023.

38. Gene Thompson, "Looking at Sports," *Bristol Herald-Courier*, September 24, 1956, 7.

39. "Jersey City's Ben Geraghty Veritable Houdini As Wichita Braves Pilot," *Jersey Journal*, August 7, 1957, 22.

40. Gene Thompson, "Looking at Sports," *Bristol Herald Courier*, May 18, 1955, 9.

41. Cy Kirtzer, "No Clock-Watchers on Front-Running Jacksonville Suns," *Buffalo News*, August 11, 1962, 24.

42. Pete Wevurski, "Clubhouse Journal," *Jersey Journal*, July 10, 1975, 7.

43. Jack Mann, "Braves Have Man for the Job, But . . ." *Newsday*, October 23, 1959, 98.

44. Bob Burnes, "Ted, Lane, Hutch Majors' Top Men," *The Sporting News*, January 1, 1958, 2.

45. Robert L. Moore, "Ben Geraghty Is Looking Ahead to Managing Big League Team," *Burlington Free Press*, June 30, 1958, 15.

46. Robert Phipps, "Stone Face, Torso Groom Braves' Stars of Tomorrow," *Evening World-Herald*, August 21, 1958, 28.

47. Johnny Carrico, "Geraghty, Despite Countenance, Has an Irish Sense of Humor; Colonels Ponder Foul Claim," *Courier-Journal*, May 9, 1959, 17.

48. Johnny Carrico, "What Magic Brought Colonels First Pennant Since 1946?" *Courier-Journal*, September 13, 1959, 71.

49. Bill Hodge, "What Kind of a Guy Was Geraghty?" *Wichita Eagle*, June 20, 1963, 41.

50. Ted Kazanski, interview with the author, March 9, 2023.

51. John DeMerit, interview with the author, March 20, 2023.

52. Tom Briere, "Geraghty Adds to Ulcer String As Colonels Avert Plane Mishap," *Minneapolis Star Tribune*, August 20, 1959, 22.

53. Joe Reichler, "Perini Says New Manager Will Be Man of Experience," *Rhinelander Daily News*, October 5, 1959, 8.

54. "Ben Geraghty Resigned to Waiting in the Wings," *Jersey Journal*, January 6, 1960, 29.

55. Mann, "Braves Have Man for the Job, But . . ."

56. DeMerit, interview.

57. Earl Ruby, "Ulcers and Baseball Don't Mix, Geraghty Finds, but Base Hits Better Than Pills As a Cure," *Courier-Journal*, June 14, 1960, 19.

58. "Ben Geraghty Plans Return Next Spring," *Jersey Journal*, August 16, 1960, 12.

59. Jordan, *A False Spring*, 200–202.

60. Jordan, *A False Spring*, 205.

61. Mike Sullivan, "Colonels of '61 Were Weird, but Happy," *Courier-Journal*, August 4, 1985, 40.

62. Howie Bedell, interview with the author, March 29, 2023.

63. Bedell, interview.

64. Fred Cranwell, "Ben Geraghty Looks Forward to Peaceful, Winning Season," *Jersey Journal*, April 3, 1961, 18.

65. Larry Henry, "Cottier Has More Than 50 Years of Memories," *Everett Herald*, February 7, 2011, www.heraldnet.com/sports/cottier-has-more-than-50-years-of-memories, accessed May 1, 2023.

66. Kazanski, interview.

67. Bedell, interview.

68. Sally John and Tommy John, *The Sally and Tommy John Story: Our Life in Baseball* (New York: Macmillan, 1983), 68.

69. John and John, *The Sally and Tommy John Story*, 68.

70. Tommy John, interview with the author, June 28, 2023.

71. John, interview.

72. Gordy Lund, interview with the author, April 24, 2023.

73. Ray Crawford, "Dedicated to Game, Geraghty Just Couldn't Stand Losing," *Miami Herald*, June 19, 1963, 23.

74. Crawford, "Dedicated to Game, Geraghty Just Couldn't Stand Losing."

75. Crawford, "Dedicated to Game, Geraghty Just Couldn't Stand Losing."

76. Wayne Minshew, "Hoyt on Look for HR No. 2." *Atlanta Constitution*, February 24, 1970, 40.

77. Morgan, letter.

78. Bedell, interview.

CHAPTER 12

1. Ken Smith, "Jack (Lucky) Lohrke," *The Sporting News*, May 5, 1948, 15.

2. Ken Smith, "Gordon on Job Every Time a Giant Falters," *The Sporting News*, June 2, 1948, 10.

3. "Fans Here Are Stunned by Sudden Shift; Reactions on Durocher Varied and Violent," *New York Times*, July 17, 1948, 9.

4. "Fans Here Are Stunned by Sudden Shift; Reactions on Durocher Varied and Violent."

5. James P. Dawson, "Lohrke to Be Used in Team's Line-up," *New York Times*, July 17, 1948, 9.

6. James P. Dawson, "Thomson, Cooper Pace 14–2 Victory," *New York Times*, July 20, 1948, 15.

7. Joel Rippel, "The 1948 Duluth Dukes Bus Crash," in *The National Pastime: Major Research on the Minor Leagues*, ed. Cecilia Tan (Phoenix, AZ: Society for American Baseball Research, 2022), https://sabr.org/journal/article/the-1948-duluth-dukes-bus-crash/, accessed July 10, 2023.

8. James P. Dawson, "Polo Grounders Top Pirates, 5–4, on Homers by Cooper and Lohrke," *New York Times*, September 3, 1948, 23.

9. "Lip Cries for Hurlers, but Clings to Hitters," *The Sporting News*, April 6, 1949, 1.

10. Joe King, "Leo the Leader Finds Stoneham the Real Boss," *The Sporting News*, April 20, 1949, 12.

11. Whitney Martin, "'Rock-Hearted' Giant Front Office Sends Jack Lohrke to Minors to Help Dick Culler Qualify for Pension," *Arizona Republic*, May 21, 1949, 8.

12. "Lohrke, Milne Express Confidence in Jersey Giants," *Bayonne Times*, July 7, 1949, 14.

13. James McGee, *The Baseball Odyssey: Volume 1—Jack Lohrke* (Small Miracles Publishing Company, 2020).

14. Herb Ashlock, "From the Bench," *Spokane Chronicle*, June 27, 1949, 15.

15. Ted Kazanski, interview with the author, March 9, 2023.

16. "Holden Replaces Jack Lohrke," *Seattle Daily Times*, June 30, 1959, 59.

17. Ron Fimrite, "O Lucky Man," *Sports Illustrated*, November 14, 1994, https://vault.si.com/vault/1994/11/14/o-lucky-man-a-twist-of-fate-saved-jack-lohrke-from-the-worst-tragedy-in-minor-league-history.

18. Jack Lohrke interview on CNN, aired July 7, 2001.

19. Fimrite, "O Lucky Man."

EPILOGUE

1. Jim Price, "Forty Years Later, Ex-Indians Look Back on Spokane's Worst Sports Tragedy," *Spokesman-Review*, June 22, 1986, 32.

2. Caren Sutton, interview with the author, February 24, 2023.

3. Jim Price, "A Half-Century of Pain," *Spokesman-Review*, June 24, 1996, 23.

4. Colleen Finney, interview with the author, June 29, 2023.

5. *Spokane Chronicle*, April 26, 1962, 37; *Spokesman-Review*, April 26, 1963, 18.

6. "Ending the Era of Harmful Native 'Themed' Mascots," www.ncai.org/proudtobe, accessed July 29, 2023.

7. "American Indians Seek to Retire Chief Illiniwek," *New York Times*, November 12, 1989, 52.

8. Jon Mooallem, "I Had a Chance to Travel Anywhere. Why Did I Pick Spokane," *New York Times*, September 21, 2021, https://www.nytimes.com/2021/09/21/magazine/spokane-indians-minor-league-baseball.html, accessed July 28, 2023.

BIBLIOGRAPHY

BOOKS, JOURNALS, AND VIDEOS

Aaron, Henry, and Lonnie Wheeler. *I Had a Hammer: The Hank Aaron Story*. New York: Harper, 1991.

Anton, Todd, and Bill Nowlin, eds. *When Baseball Went to War*. Chicago: Triumph Books, 2008.

Appel, Marty. *Casey Stengel: Baseball's Greatest Character*. New York: Doubleday, 2017.

Beevor, Antony. *Ardennes 1944: The Battle of the Bulge*. New York: Penguin Random House, 2015.

Cohen, Joel H. *Hammerin' Hank of the Braves*. New York: Scholastic, 1971.

Dobbins, Dick. *The Grand Minor League: An Oral History of the Old Pacific Coast League*. Emeryville, CA: Woodford Press, 1999.

John, Sally, and Tommy John. *The Sally and Tommy John Story: Our Life in Baseball*. New York: Macmillan, 1983.

Jordan, Pat. *A False Spring*. New York: Dodd, Mead, 1975.

McGee, James. *The Baseball Odyssey: Volume 1—Jack Lohrke*. Small Miracles Publishing, 2020.

Mohr, Mark, director. *Spokane Indians: A Century of Baseball*. Peak Video Productions, 2003. 55 min, VHS.

Popejoy, Don, and Penny Hutten. *Images of America: Early Spokane*. Charleston, SC: Arcadia Publishing, 2010.

Presenting the 35th Infantry Division in World War II, 1941–1945. Albert Love Enterprises, 1946.

Rippel, Joel. "The 1948 Duluth Dukes Bus Crash." In *The National Pastime: Major Research on the Minor Leagues*, edited by Cecilia Tan. Phoenix, AZ: Society for American Baseball Research, 2022.

Weintraub, Robert. *The Victory Season: The End of World War II and the Birth of Baseball's Golden Age*. New York: Hachette, 2013.

ARCHIVAL NEWSPAPERS AND MAGAZINES

Arizona Republic
Asbury Park Press
Atlanta Constitution
Bayonne Times
Bellingham Herald
Bend Bulletin
Bergen Evening Record
Bessemer Herald
Boston Globe
Boys' Life
Bradenton Herald
Bristol Herald Courier
Brooklyn Daily Eagle
Brooklyn Times-Union
Buffalo News
Burlington Free Press
Charlotte Observer
Courier-Journal (Louisville, KY)
Courier-News (Plainfield, NJ)
Daily News (New York)
Daily Press (Newport News, VA)
Daily Register (Red Bank, NJ)
Deseret News
El Paso Herald Post
Evansville Press
Evening Sun (Hanover, PA)
Evening World-Herald (Omaha, NE)
Everett Herald
Fort Worth Star-Telegram
Indianapolis Star

Jersey Journal
Kansas City Times
Lake Geneva Regional News
Los Angeles Times
Metropolitan Pasadena Star-News
Miami Herald
Minneapolis Star Tribune
Modesto Bee
Montreal Gazette
Montreal Star
Morning Call (Allentown, PA)
New York Times
Newsday (New York)
Nashua Telegraph
Oakland Tribune
Ogden Standard-Examiner
Ottawa Journal
Pasadena Post
Philadelphia Inquirer
Post-Register (Idaho Falls, ID)
Press-Democrat (Santa Rosa, CA)
Rhinelander Daily News
Sacramento Bee
Salt Lake Tribune
San Diego Union
San Francisco Chronicle
San Francisco Examiner
Seattle Post-Intelligencer
Seattle Star
Seattle Times
Selma Times-Journal
Spokane Chronicle
Spokesman-Review
The Sporting News
Sports Illustrated
Stockton Evening and Sunday Record
Tacoma News Tribune
Tampa Times
Tampa Tribune

Times-Advocate (Escondido, CA)
Times-News (Twin Falls, ID)
Tucson Daily Citizen
Vancouver Sun
Wichita Beacon
Wichita Eagle
Wilkes-Barre Times Leader

WEB SITES

ancestry.com
baseballhall.org
baseballinwartime.com
baseball-reference.com
chevronsanddiamonds.wordpress.com
coulthart.com
militaryyearbookproject.org
newspapers.com
sabr.org
spokanetribe.com
vault.si.com
worldwartwoveterans.org

INDEX

ABOUT THE AUTHOR

Eric Vickrey is the author of *Runnin' Redbirds: The World Champion 1982 St. Louis Cardinals*. He has contributed to numerous publications as a member of the Society for American Baseball Research. Born and raised in Illinois, he now lives in Washington State.